THE WEEK OF THE JELLYHOPPERS

An adventure for Jane

Written by Pauline Cartwright
Illustrated by Martin Bailey

© 1995 Shortland Publications Inc.

03 02 01 00 99 98
11 10 9 8 7 6 5 4 3

All rights reserved.

Published by Shortland Publications Inc.
Produced by Shortland Publications,
2B Cawley Street, Ellerslie, Auckland, New Zealand.

Distributed in the United States of America by

a division of Reed Elsevier Inc.
500 Coventry Lane
Crystal Lake, IL 60014
800-822-8661

Distributed in Canada by

PRENTICE HALL GINN
1870 Birchmount Road
Scarborough
Ontario M1P 2J7

Printed through Bookbuilders Limited, Hong Kong.

ISBN: 0-7901-0986-7

Contents

Chapter 1	6
Chapter 2	12
Chapter 3	18
Chapter 4	26
Chapter 5	32
Chapter 6	39
Chapter 7	48
Chapter 8	56
Chapter 9	62
Chapter 10	71
Chapter 11	78
Chapter 12	85
Chapter 13	93
Chapter 14	101
Chapter 15	110
Chapter 16	117

The Mor...

Saturday, July 6   Establi...

UFO Sighting in

RIBBONWOOD. "It was a dome-shaped craft, about as large as a house," said Mr. John Rogers, a Ribbonwood farmhand. "It had bright green, flashing lights."

Mr. Rogers was describing the UFO he claims that he saw descending onto a local property last night. The 20-year-old was one of two witnesses to what some have described as "an interplanetary visit."

Scientists have yet to respond to the claim. An investigative team from the Arawera Research Station says it plans to examine the area where the purported sighting occurred: a field on Mr. Tom Richards' Ribbonwood farm.

A wide swathe of Mr. Richards' potato crop has been singed black on its upper leaves. In the center, where there is a completely bare patch of soil, Mr. Rogers said he saw the craft deposit several large objects at around 11:30 last night.

He led his employer, Mr Richards, to the area, and both men claim they saw two small heaps of "twisted, smoking metal" where the bare patch now shows in the crop.

"The craft seemed to be i trouble – I saw tongues of flam

Crops Face Bumper Yea

ing Star

★★★

1919 Volume LXXVI

Ribbonwood

shooting from one side," said Mr. Rogers. "After the metal pieces had been jettisoned, the vessel rose back into the air, and there were no more flames."

Air traffic controllers in the surrounding area have been unable to offer an explanation, or to establish that any craft had a flight path over the Ribbonwood area. They will be meeting with other air personnel at the Richards' property today.

Ribbonwood Sheriff Arnold O'Shea said that just before being called to the farm by Mr. Richards, he was struck by a sight in the sky. **cont. page 24**

Bank Finds New President

Chapter 1

Isobel's father, Mr. Miro, couldn't believe what he was reading in the paper. "Well, at least they haven't called it a 'flying saucer.' I always thought that was a stupid name."

Margery Hopgood, part-time baby-sitter, part-time housekeeper for Isobel and her father, stopped her energetic Saturday morning cleaning. "Farther down in the article, Sheriff O'Shea says that it was shaped like a hat. Sort of like a bowler hat. So I suppose they couldn't really call it a saucer."

"A flying hat," said Isobel, poking at the sliminess of her poached egg. "They could have called it a flying hat."

"There'll be some explanation," said Mr. Miro. "Just some ordinary thing that seemed extraordinary at the time."

Mrs. Hopgood looked slightly put out. The story was exciting! What's more, it put small-town Ribbonwood on the map. Mr. Miro was new to the town, but that didn't give him the right to suggest some of its residents were wild storytellers, or people who didn't know what they were seeing. "John Rogers is a pleasant young man. He'd have no reason to make up a story. And I've read before of UFOs that have never been explained. They have got the evidence this time, too. I mean, look at that photo! Look at those potatoes!"

"Probably blight," said Mr. Miro wryly.

"Mr. Richards is an honest man." Mrs. Hopgood's offended air was now very obvious.

"I'm sure he is," Mr. Miro reassured her. "I'm sure he is. Isobel, finish your egg. We'll go up to this farm and have a look. Have a chat with the locals. We'll come back and tell you all about it, Margery."

"I heard a noise last night before you got home, Dad. A sort of whining noise."

Mrs. Hopgood looked triumphant and impressed at the same time. She had been baby-sitting while Mr. Miro was at a meeting at the Community Center. "I must have had the TV up too loud to hear it. But that's just what they say in the paper. They say it made a sort of whining noise!"

Isobel remembered how the knot of loneliness tightening inside her had meant she was unable to sleep. She had wished that there had been the swish of cars going by, for even that would have seemed like some kind of company. But their new home was right on the edge of the small town and there was little traffic. It was great that her father had gotten the bank manager's job, but it was awful to be nearly eleven years old and friendless in yet another new town, the third in the last six years.

"I thought it was a dog," said Isobel. She had sat up and twitched back the curtain to peer across the fields below the clear night sky. "I didn't actually look up."

"You might have seen it if you had. Think of that!" said Mrs. Hopgood, and she polished the brass candlestick with a vigor that made it shine as much as the delighted smile on her face.

"Could we have a dog?" Isobel suddenly piped up.

"You've asked that before – about seven hundred and sixty-five times before, in fact. No," said her father. "Now, hurry up. We'll shoot up to this farm before there are too many people there."

A dog, thought Isobel, wouldn't have to be left behind if she and Dad had to move again. She wouldn't have to explain who she was to a dog as she had to with people. "I'm coming," she said, poking the remains of her egg under a crust. "If we had a dog, he could have come, too. For the walk."

"You might get to talk to the scientists!" Mrs. Hopgood said to her, thrilled at the importance of such a thought. "They'll want to talk to everyone who saw or heard anything. Anything at all."

"It was probably just a dog," said Isobel. "Anyway, I don't want to talk to anyone."

Mr. Miro narrowed his eyes a little, the way he did when he was slightly worried. "Of course you do. Oh, not the scientists, of course. But you might meet some of the children who'll be in your class when school starts."

Isobel wished her father wouldn't mention school. The thought of another whole roomful of strange children, was more than she could stand.

There was already quite a crowd at the Richards' farm. Isobel couldn't help feeling some of the excitement in the air. At first it was difficult to believe that adults were saying and believing the things she was hearing around her.

"He'd been working late, you see. Fixing the tractor. Looked up at the stars as he came out of the shed, and there it was."

"Tom Richards said the metal was still smoking when he went out."

"Hadn't believed John till he saw that, had he?"

"Where is it now, then? That's what I want to know."

"Arnold O'Shea said there was a noise before he saw the flames."

"He was out in his car. Saw the thing in the sky. Like a hat, he said. Shaped like a hat, with lights all around it."

"It was losing altitude when it came over the farm as though it was in trouble. John Rogers reckoned he nearly froze with fright."

"Well, wouldn't you, if you saw it? Probably thought little green men were going to leap out and grab him!"

The blackened area of potato crop had been roped off, but the sight of it was sufficient to keep the curious crowd speculating about what might and might not have happened. They might, Isobel thought, be there until sunset.

But only forty-five minutes after she and her father had arrived, Isobel left and slipped off home.

The whole idea of an alien craft visiting

Ribbonwood had seemed to her at first quite silly. She knew her father thought it was. But now Isobel knew it was true, that a spacecraft had come in the night, that John Rogers did speak the truth. For she was carrying home proof of the visit.

She had, wrapped in her cardigan, a creature from outer space.

Chapter 2

She, Isobel Miro, three-week resident of Ribbonwood, was custodian of the only space creature on Earth! It was quite a terrifying responsibility when she thought about it. If someone discovered her secret – for she had decided she was definitely going to keep it a secret – would she be in serious trouble? Was it against the law to hide an extraterrestrial being? Would she be able to care for it? What did it eat, besides chocolate?

While she was at the Richards' farm, Isobel had been sitting on a log by one of the farm sheds, nibbling on a chocolate bar. It was then that she heard the purring noise. Parting the dry grass at her feet, she found two beautiful, long-lashed brown eyes looking up at her. They were not the eyes of a cat.

The eyes had an almost human appearance, although they were not as large, and seemed to be set in a body rather than in a face. Or was it, the astonished Isobel wondered, that they were set in a face and that there was no body?

Seeing no reason to be afraid, Isobel crouched down to look more closely. The body (Isobel decided it was definitely a body) was slightly larger than that of a porcupine and about the same shape. But while a porcupine is covered with unfriendly prickles, this creature was smooth and shining and the most beautiful glowing shade of green. It was almost like mint jelly poured out of a jar, but its green shading was more vivid and alive, the color of new shoots of grass. Gently, Isobel reached out her hand. The creature didn't shy away, but slid its warm, smooth body over it.

"Where have you come from, and what are you?" murmured Isobel. "Are you called a jelly-animal? You are a beautiful thing."

The purring noise had ceased for a moment, as the creature slid over her hand. Isobel realized that there was no longer a trace of melted chocolate on her fingers. Maybe it was the smell of chocolate that had made it first appear.

Isobel held out a piece. The creature

immediately slid the front portion of its body over her fingers, and the chocolate was gone. Where was its mouth? For that matter, where was its nose?

It might not like being turned over and examined. It might run away. What does it run on? Isobel wondered.

She edged back, holding a piece of chocolate in her open hand. The creature slid forward a little. Isobel laughed with delight at the glowing creature that showed no fear. She edged back more, and then jumped in surprise as the animal sprang twice into the air and landed at her feet on top of her fallen cardigan.

"You clever creature! You hop! And without any feet. Jelly-animal isn't a good enough name. I'm going to call you a *jellyhopper*."

"Hello," said a voice suddenly. "Who are you talking to?"

With one swift movement, Isobel scooped the creature up in her cardigan, clutched it against her body, and hoped desperately that the jellyhopper wouldn't object to being half-crushed. She whirled around.

A girl about her own age stood in front of her. She was very pretty, with blond hair and wide eyes. The blue shirt above her shorts was exactly the color of her eyes, which Isobel decided were very curious. No, more than curious. They were *nosy.*

"I'm not talking to anyone," said Isobel.

The blond girl looked disbelieving. Isobel assumed a high and mighty air, which she knew from past experience other children found unpleasant. "Well, can you see anyone here to talk to?" she demanded. "I certainly can't."

"You were talking," snapped the blond girl. "You said something about hopping."

Isobel clutched her cardigan a little closer, feeling the creature inside squirm a little. "Hopping!" echoed Isobel in the most regal tone she could muster. "How very ridiculous!"

She turned her back, stalked back to the log, and hoped that her rudeness would discourage any more conversation. In the silence, Isobel longed to sneak a glance over her shoulder.

"Well, I must say," said the girl's voice suddenly, "you're the stupidest girl I've ever met. You are probably so stupid that you don't even know a UFO was here last night. You probably don't even know what a UFO is."

Isobel turned around enough to watch the blond girl striding angrily away. Then she smiled to herself. That was it! The UFO! This strange creature came from the spacecraft! Carefully, Isobel undid her bundled cardigan. The astonishing green animal looked unharmed.

"Poor little lost jellyhopper," cooed Isobel. "I'm sorry to have squashed you like that when you're so far from home. Now, since you've got no friends and I've got no friends, we'd better stick together. I'm going to take you home."

Wrapping the jellyhopper more carefully this time, along with two squares of chocolate that she hoped were somewhere near its invisible mouth, Isobel ran to find her father and tell him she was going home.

He looked slightly surprised. "Wouldn't you rather stay and play with some of the children until I'm ready to go?"

Isobel blushed a little, remembering her rudeness to the blond girl. But her father, deep in conversation with a tall, dark man, didn't try to dissuade her further. Isobel ran off before the jellyhopper began to squirm.

Isobel paused once to unwrap the jellyhopper enough so that its eyes could gaze out. "And so that you can breathe with your invisible nose. I suppose you have to breathe like everyone else."

Later, on a quiet stretch of road, she paused to set it down on the roadside. When she walked off briskly, the creature hopped along behind her, somewhat like an oval, green bouncing ball. Then the sound of an approaching car made her scoop it up again, and she carried it the rest of the way.

Chapter 3

Every now and then as she walked toward home, Isobel felt a shiver of excitement ripple right through her. What if right this minute she went walking down to the newspaper office, or to the police station, and said, "I'd like to report the discovery of a space creature"?

She'd be famous. They'd take photos of her holding her jellyhopper. She'd be on television. The whole world would hear about her. All the kids in every school she'd gone to would stare in wonder.

She liked school, but she dreaded starting at Ribbonwood – starting again, having to try to smile at people she didn't know, and having a lot of strange faces ask her curious questions. Maybe nobody would want to be friends with her.

They would if she was famous. Everyone would want to know her if she was known all over the world as the girl who had discovered the first space creature on Earth.

At Mason's Flat, Maria had been her friend for awhile. But Maria moved, leaving Isobel feeling alone again. Before that, in Opito, she remembered that she and Rebecca Stone had played together a lot. But she was only a little kid then, only seven. Isobel dreamed of a friend that she would know for years and years, a friend with whom she could laugh and talk and tell secrets. She didn't want to be "the new girl" ever again.

Being famous would mean she was known by everybody before she even went to school. Then the shivers of excitement were replaced by shivers of apprehension. If she reported her find, the jellyhopper would be taken away. It would be caged so that scientists could study it. They might even do experiments on it.

Isobel made up her mind. "I'm not going to tell anyone about you," she said to the creature. "Not now. Perhaps later when I've really thought about it, but not now. You're going to be my secret. I'm not even going to tell Dad."

The Miros' new home, set on the edge of town, was a little too large for just Isobel and her father.

Mr. Miro muttered about "waste of space." Isobel, knowing that he was in some way referring to all the unexpected nooks and crannies, liked the house. The bay window seat in the sprawling hallway was perfect for curling up on in the sunshine. The closet under the stairway was excitingly dark and roomy. The whole house felt cozy, as if it had been loved by many people.

The yard at the back of the property was large and untidy. Unpruned orchard trees leaned their arms out over some ancient sheds. Mr. Miro talked of getting rid of the sheds, but in the meantime, Isobel found them a great place to play. Now, she darted along the side of the house toward them. Slipping through the second doorway, she let it close behind her. The shed was dim, after the bright sunlight outside. Isobel sat herself on an old fruit box and set the jellyhopper down. "I hope you don't mind dust," she murmured.

The jellyhopper sat placidly at her feet.

"Don't you want to explore?" Isobel picked it up and stroked it gently, while she tried to make some order out of the whirl of thoughts in her head.

Imagine her, Isobel Miro, caring for a creature from another planet. It was like being in a strange and very exciting dream. She wondered whether on its own planet the creature was a pet, or whether it had some other special purpose. The jellyhopper slid around in her lap so smoothly that had she not been watching it, she felt she wouldn't have noticed. The warm, brown eyes blinked with their long lashes.

Suddenly, it jumped off her lap and started exploring the shed. Sometimes it slid. Sometimes it hopped, and Isobel laughed as puffs of dust flew up.

"I think you're a male," said Isobel, "so I'll give you a boy's name." She tried several out loud. Daniel seemed too serious. Toby wasn't serious enough. Thomas came closer. The hopper did a few jumps toward a corner. Isobel giggled. "I could call you after our housekeeper – Mrs. Hopgood. It sort of fits."

Head bent on hands, she thought some more – and suddenly she knew his name. "Obadiah! That's who you'll be. Obadiah. It has exactly the right sort of sound."

From now on, life was certainly going to have added excitement. It was an enormous responsibility to be the custodian of the only known space creature on Earth. Isobel ached to have someone with whom she could share it.

Her father was calling her. Isobel whispered, "Stay here, Obadiah. Please stay here. I'll be back. I promise." Leaving the second-to-last piece of chocolate in the far corner of the shed, she slipped out the door.

On Saturdays, Isobel didn't mind that she was supposed to help Mrs. Hopgood with the chores, but there hadn't been much time this morning.

"It's been an exciting morning, but jobs still have to be done," said her father. "Time to clean your room."

"It sure has been exciting," agreed Isobel. "Dad, do you think there were any creatures on that UFO?"

"Creatures!" Her father laughed. "If there *was* a UFO. I find it all a bit hard to swallow. It's beyond belief. And yet those blackened potatoes…" He shook his head again. "Metal heaps don't fall out of the sky and then disappear. They'll probably find it was a meteorite or something."

Isobel was no longer listening. She had forgotten about the metal John Rogers said had fallen from the craft. That would be when Obadiah arrived! Arrived was hardly the word. Hurtled would be more like it, although people usually talked about things hurtling into space, not out of space. Obadiah must be very tough to fall and stay unharmed. For a fleeting moment, she wondered if he could fly.

"You're not worried are you, Izzy?" asked her father. "Not frightened with these questions about creatures?"

"Oh, no," hastened Isobel. "I just thought – well – someone has to drive a spaceship, and there could have been other creatures along – "

Her father laughed. "A Noah's ark from space, full of furry snakes and ducks with cat's feet. Now go and clean your room."

Later, Isobel organized the Saturday lunch because Mrs. Hopgood had left early, eager to call at the Richards' farm and share in all the excitement. As she boiled eggs, chopped up tomatoes, and shredded lettuce leaves, Isobel put a portion of each food aside in a paper bag. She added other items – a handful of raisins, a slice of bread, a piece of sausage.

Around midafternoon, Isobel tried feeding Obadiah. She placed all the collected foods out in a long row. "A jellyhopper's smorgasbord," she announced with a flourish.

Obadiah slid around and in between all the items, but didn't touch one. Nor did he show any interest in water.

Isobel was tempted to tell her secret to her father. She couldn't allow Obadiah to die. However, he *did* look all right at the moment. He was the same color, he glowed the same, he was just as active. Isobel gave a small moan of worry. A space creature was an enormous responsibility. And hiding him wasn't simple.

Her father was calling her outside. She thrust Obadiah under a box, and raced to the door. Her father scolded her about not being out in the fresh air and told her they were going visiting that night.

"Dad, do I have to go?"

"Of course you do. They've got a daughter who will be in your class at school, and some other children. You'll enjoy it."

But Isobel didn't enjoy it. Mr. and Mrs. Morrow were very nice. Mrs. Morrow had a soft, kind smile that was real, not just a baring of teeth, as smiles were with some people. Mr. Morrow seemed to get along very well with her dad.

The woman introduced as Sue seemed nice, too. Isobel's small face in its curtain of black hair had stared boldly at Sue. It happened quite often that when they went out to visit, there would be an extra woman there. Her father sometimes went out with the woman later, but usually only a few times. Still, Isobel felt duty-bound to check such people out.

Then a cute little roly-poly boy of about three came toddling in, an older boy of about six, and the blond girl Isobel had been rude to at the farm.

The adults took their quietness for shyness, and eventually they were all sent off to the games room, where Angela Morrow said, in unsympathetic tones, "My mother said I've got to be nice to you because your mother's dead."

"Well, in that case," said Isobel sharply, "I'm glad yours is alive, because I don't have to bother being nice to you."

She spent most of the evening playing with the roly-poly boy until he had to go to bed. She was hoping that Obadiah, hiding out under his box in the shed, was safe and happy. She wished her father would stop talking so much to that Sue woman so that they could go home.

Chapter 4

One of Isobel's reasons for wanting to find out what else the creature ate was so that he would stay. If he became hungry, he was bound to go looking elsewhere for food, and maybe he would never return.

When her father asked if she wanted to go back to the Richards' farm on Sunday morning, she told him she wanted to stay home. There had been a brief item on Saturday night's news about the supposed spacecraft sighting. On Sunday morning, a TV crew was going to film at the farm and interview witnesses.

"I could appear with you and really surprise them," Isobel told Obadiah. She took him up to the kitchen instead. It was theirs to explore – Mrs. Hopgood was not coming in.

She put out potatoes on the floor, some cooked and some raw. She tried cheese, condensed milk, spaghetti, bananas, carrots, and cookies. Obadiah hovered over the last a little while, but in the end, as he had done with the other foods, he slid off without touching it.

Isobel scooped him up and held him in front of an open cupboard. "What do you eat?" she asked in despair. Obadiah began to purr, and she felt his warm, sleek body wriggle. The purring became almost a hum. "Excitement makes you hum," murmured Isobel. "What's in there that makes you excited?"

Not flour, not pudding mix. Chocolate chips! A floor trail of them was rapidly demolished. Isobel put almost the entire remainder in her pocket to feed him later. She tucked the nearly empty package far back in the cupboard.

Isobel spent a portion of the afternoon experimenting to see if Obadiah had intelligence. "Come, Obadiah," she would say, holding out some chocolate chips.

Obediently, he would respond. But with nothing in her hand, he seemed to have no idea he was being called.

"It could be that you are very stupid," said Isobel, slightly offended that only food, and not her commands, attracted the jellyhopper.

"I wonder what you did on your other planet. And why did they have you in the spacecraft?"

Because she didn't know any of the people who had been interviewed that day at the farm, she found the evening news boring. The interviewer appeared to be trying to make John Rogers, Mr. Richards, and Sheriff O'Shea look like fanciful storytellers, treating their experience as a joke.

"It's true, you silly man!" said Isobel angrily to the television set.

Her father looked around. "You don't know that, Izzy."

Isobel wanted to say that she did, but instead, she asked if she could go for a walk in the fields behind the house. "I won't be long."

She raced down to the back of the yard and opened the shed. "Come on, Obadiah." She held out a handful of chocolate chips. "We're going for a walk."

Maybe there was something in the outdoor world that Obadiah ate. Just in case she met someone, she decided to carry him in a small backpack. She let Obadiah slide over it before she hooked it on her shoulder. "I'll put you in there if there's anyone around. So don't be surprised."

The evening was still and warm. Isobel liked the soft swish of grass against her bare legs.

Across the open field the land dipped down into a shallow valley and some beech trees grew there. Isobel had climbed one of them the first week she had moved to Ribbonwood.

Isobel and her strange friend ambled across the field toward the beech grove. "Now if you feel like eating anything, please do," said Isobel, as though she were talking to an aunt who had come for afternoon tea. Then she sighed. Apart from grass, weeds, and a few flowers thrusting their heads up, there wasn't really much from which to choose.

"You don't eat worms, do you? Or bugs?" Isobel skipped a little way and called back to Obadiah. "I think you're dumb, you know. I'm sure you don't know why we're out here."

In the shade of the beech trees, it was cool and dry. Obadiah sat still when Isobel swung on a low branch. He showed no interest in a leaf that she tugged off and tossed to him, so she threw him a few chocolate chips.

She sauntered up the low valley, which looked as if it might hold a stream in its base in the winter. One or two ferns grew in damp patches. There was another small grove of beeches ahead and, at the back of them, an old barn that looked unused.

"Obadiah –" She turned and couldn't see the

jellyhopper. "Obadiah, where are you?"

She reached into her pocket, clutching for a handful of chips. She held them on an open palm, crouching low and turning in a circle. "Come, Obadiah. Come here."

Then she saw a flash of green quite a distance ahead. It was Obadiah, hopping fast toward the barn. Isobel closed her hands on the chips and ran after him. "Where are you going?"

As she caught up, she could hear him humming. He was excited. Was there something there that he could eat? What loud humming. Excited now herself, Isobel trailed behind Obadiah as he skirted the old barn, sliding along its edges as if trying to find a way in.

"I'll open the door." She ran ahead of Obadiah and pushed. The door was heavy. Obadiah slid between her feet and, with a wriggle, disappeared through the gap as it opened. Isobel pushed harder. The door creaked open, and Isobel was startled by the noise, by the loud, humming noise. It couldn't all be coming from Obadiah.

Then her eyes, adjusting to the darkness, nearly popped out of her head. Obadiah wasn't the only space creature on Earth! The barn was full of them! Or so it seemed at first glance. Red, yellow, and green shapes hopped around the barn and hummed with such excitement that the noise was almost overwhelming.

Chapter 5

Isobel hung on to the doorpost. How had they come to be here? So many of them! No wonder Obadiah was excited. Here were so many of his own kind. Or was it so many?

The humming quieted to a soft, united purring. The creatures were sliding from place to place instead of hopping. Isobel slowly moved forward from the door. No, the barn wasn't full of jellyhoppers. There must be about seven – no, eight of them, Isobel thought, as she tried to count the moving shapes. None was quite as large as Obadiah.

"But you're all so beautiful." Isobel reached down to slide a hand over a warm, red hopper. Another, as yellow as sunshine, slid by. "Where did you come from? Who put you here?"

Isobel stood up suddenly. Who indeed had put them in here? She, Isobel Miro, thought she was the only person in Ribbonwood – in fact, in the whole world – who had a space creature in her keeping. Here was a barn with a bunch of them, and that meant someone must have put them there. Isobel moved to the door. Who owned this barn, and had the owners put the jellyhoppers in here? She peered outside, as if the owners might suddenly reveal themselves. The creatures must have come from the same spaceship as Obadiah. When and where had they been found?

In the last two days, it seemed to Isobel, her head had been filled with one question after another. Finding the answers wasn't easy.

She turned back to the barn interior. "What do you all eat, anyway?" she demanded.

The jellyhoppers took no notice. She crouched on her hands and knees and coaxed Obadiah to her by rolling two or three chocolate chips in her fingertips. "Come outside with me a moment, Obadiah, and let's think about this."

She picked him up and walked to the door. There was no sound, but the rest of the creatures slid along behind. Isobel didn't try to stop them. She knew that she could coax them all back in again with chocolate.

Outside the barn she put Obadiah on the ground and watched with some delight as the eight other hoppers slid or hopped around on the grass. They were so different from anything she had ever seen in her life. Those brown, brown eyes in their colored, glowing bodies. "You're all so beautiful." Isobel danced a step or two in enjoyment.

"You all like chocolate, don't you?" Two red hoppers slid quickly over the chips she put on the grass. A yellow one followed them.

"THEY'RE GONE!"

The cry came from inside the barn, and Isobel leaped as high, she was sure, as a jellyhopper.

"The door's open!" It was another voice, and it came from inside the barn, too. Whoever was there must have come in from the back.

"The door's open – wide open!"

Not knowing who was coming, Isobel rushed to protect what was hers. Deftly, she scooped up Obadiah as he slid by her feet, and she stood clutching him as three faces appeared at the barn door.

One was a girl about her own age with freckles and brown hair. The other two were boys. One was probably the girl's younger brother, as his face, although fatter, looked like hers and his hair was a similar brown. The other boy, whose serious expression Isobel found rather intimidating, looked a year or two older.

The younger boy spoke first. "They're here. It's OK. They haven't gone."

Isobel saw a look of relief pass over the girl's face. The older boy's serious expression changed to one of anger, as he saw Isobel standing with Obadiah clutched in her arms. "What are you doing here? Why are you touching things that don't belong to you? Put it down."

Did this boy suppose that Obadiah was theirs? Isobel felt anger rising inside her, and her face tightened.

The girl looked uncomfortable. "It's all right, Jamie. They're here. The bouncers are here. We'll –"

"Shut up, Ruth." The boy spoke sharply; then turning to Isobel, he said, "These bouncers are ours. You've got no right opening that door. No right coming here in the first place."

Ruth was glancing about as the jellyhoppers slithered through the grass. "There're eight, Jamie. They're all here on the grass." She pointed at Isobel. "That's the ninth one. She's got another one! It's bigger than ours!"

"Don't be stupid, Ruth. Just count right. Oh, don't bother. Let's get them back inside. And you," he glared at Isobel, "had better give us that back!"

How dare this boy assume Obadiah was his!

How dare he glare and accuse and demand. How dare he not listen to the girl, who obviously had some sense. Isobel glared back. "I most certainly will not give him back. And for your information, he is not a "that". His name is Obadiah, and he belongs to me."

The younger boy was dashing around the grass, trying to scoop up the jellyhoppers, which kept slithering out of his grasp. "We have to get them back inside! They might escape – and then everyone will know!"

"Stop grabbing at them, Reuben," said Ruth. "You could frighten them half to death."

"You had no right to open this door!" The boy called Jamie glared again at Isobel.

He moved towards her. Isobel was seized by a sudden fear. There was only one of her, and there were three of them.

"My jellyhopper came here by himself," she said, using her high and mighty voice. At the same time, she began stepping back away from the three children. "And if I were you and had this many jellyhoppers to look after, I'd do it properly. I'd train them for a start."

Still walking backwards while the three somewhat-confused children stared at her, she groped in her pocket for the last of the chocolate chips. Obadiah gave a wriggle as she passed the handful in front of him. Placing him on the ground, she turned her back on the three children. With her cupped palm turned so that the children couldn't see it, but so that she knew Obadiah would smell the chips, she spoke in firm, confident tones. "Come, Obadiah. Home."

As she ran, the jellyhopper leaped along behind her, and Isobel had the satisfaction of hearing Ruth say to the others, "I told you it was another one. Hey, I wonder how she's trained it."

orning Star

Established 1919 ★★★ **Volume LXXVI**

SCIENTISTS CONSIDER SPACECRAFT "EVIDENCE"

RIBBONWOOD. Claims over the weekend of a UFO sighting in Ribbonwood are being investigated by a group of scientists from the Arawera Research Station.

On the night of July 5, when the alleged spacecraft was seen, there were no scheduled air flights over the region. The investigative team has not yet delivered an official statement.

"We have further inspections to make," said Arawera scientist Dr. Stanley Chang. "Studies as to the cause of the burned effect in the potato crop have proved inconclusive."

Local sheriff Arnold O'Shea was one of two Ribbonwood residents who claimed to have sighted the unidentified flying object.

He has asked for further visitors to the site of the alleged landing to refrain from entering the area.

"Mr. Richards would appreciate people respecting the fact that his farm is private property," said Sheriff O'Shea. "There is a scientific investigation being carried out here. It does not require an audience," he said. **cont. page 4**

Chapter 6

"They say there've been hundreds at the Richards' farm." Mrs. Hopgood's head peered around the laundry door, where she was supposedly doing the washing. "I was up there myself in the morning – well, you were, too, weren't you, Paul? I never went back in the afternoon, but they say there were hordes of people! You would have noticed the cars around the place, even if you weren't there."

"Yes," said Mr. Miro vaguely, as he scanned the paper and ate his morning toast. Isobel knew he didn't like involved conversations over the breakfast table. She supposed it was something to do with getting his head ready for a day at the bank.

"My neighbor was on television. Did you see

her?" Mrs. Hopgood didn't wait for an answer. "I was nearly on. The camera just missed me. There wasn't much to photograph, of course. No little green men or anything. The whole thing is such a mystery. Why would a spacecraft come here? That's the thing I keep asking. Why would it come here? It's a bit scary, really. Like all the strangers in town."

Mr. Miro looked up, and spoke rather sharply. "Margery, something somebody thought they saw is nothing at all to be alarmed about." He flashed a sudden smile at Isobel. "Is it now?"

Isobel knew he was worried Mrs. Hopgood might frighten her. "I don't think so," she said cheerfully. "I don't think so at all."

Her father seemed reassured, and returned to the paper as he muttered, "All the strangers hanging around are another thing."

Isobel risked a morning question over the watery sounds now coming from the laundry, where Mrs. Hopgood had finally retreated. An ordinary question about ordinary things might help calm down the mad carousel of thoughts that twirled in her head. "What's wrong with a lot of people around?"

"It's good in one way," said Mr. Miro. "I guess the sale of ice-cream cones has definitely gone up. But I wasn't thrilled with the look of some of those people. Now this afternoon – "

Mrs. Hopgood was obviously still listening. Her head popped around the laundry door again. "I'll stay till one o'clock. You'll be home for lunch until two. Isobel can come to my place after that, if you like."

Isobel made a face. "I'm all right here. I'm not five years old."

Her father frowned. "Margery, I'll phone you at lunchtime and let you know." He left the table and picked up his briefcase. "I'll be glad when school starts."

I won't be, thought Isobel darkly; but the thought didn't linger long among the million other thoughts. She had never before had so much to think about. The excitement and the worry and the responsibility and the anticipation were incredible. Even if she had been having a birthday, a slumber party, and a new school to cope with all on the same day, it would have been only half as incredible and agonizing, she was sure.

Obadiah had spent the night in her bedroom. It didn't seem to worry him that she thrust him under the blankets whenever she thought her father might be popping his head in to check on her, or to say good night. She found that in the dark, he glowed just enough for her to be able to see him wherever he was in the room. It was almost like having a comforting night-light, like the one she had when she was little.

She had taken him into her room after she came back from her walk, fearful that the excitement he had displayed on discovering others of his kind could mean he might try to return to them. Isobel didn't want that bossy boy having the chance to claim Obadiah as his.

She wondered again, as she wondered in the night, whether there were other jellyhoppers elsewhere, as well as in the barn. Perhaps they were creatures that the people from the other planet didn't want. Perhaps they were dumping them on Earth to get rid of them. But Isobel didn't think so, now that she had discovered the remarkable ability that Obadiah had.

Just before Isobel meant to turn out her light, Obadiah in his journeying around the room had given a hop that took him to the edge of a pile of paper. It tumbled and fluttered from the bookshelf to the floor.

Isobel climbed out of bed to pick it up. "You silly thing, Obadiah. You should be sliding, not hopping. Bedrooms aren't – " Her voice faltered, then stopped, as she saw something unbelievable happening.

As if he had heard and understood her words, Obadiah was moving now by sliding around the floor. He slid over a blank sheet of the tumbled paper and, as he did so, there appeared from beneath him an image on the paper. Isobel blinked. The paper had been blank. It definitely had been blank – and now there was a strange, involved diagram on it. The lines of it appeared to glow slightly, and Isobel had a sudden but fleeting fear that the pinkish red shine might burst into flames. She stared at the peculiar diagram, and then stared at Obadiah.

Obadiah slid over her foot. Isobel drew it back quickly, half-expecting a strange, shining diagram to appear on her foot, like a wondrous tattoo. Then, unable to believe what she had just seen happen, she grabbed a blank sheet of paper, thrust it in Obadiah's path, and watched as another diagram appeared. She did it again and again. But the fifth time, the sheet of paper stayed blank.

Isobel picked up the four sheets with the diagrams. They were all different. They were not of anything she could understand. And they were labeled in places with symbols that Isobel had never seen before.

Somehow, Isobel found what had happened

quite scary. Obadiah, her jellyhopper, had been a quaint, brown-eyed pet – a cute, harmless creature filling a gap in her life. Now he had become something else, a link with the people from whose planet he had come. Isobel could cope with a space creature; but aliens who drew complex, faintly shining plans were another thing. Isobel was quite sure that people had drawn them. Obadiah was simply the carrier.

Excited by, yet frightened of, the strange, glowing pictures, Isobel thrust them in a drawer and climbed into bed. Then, all at once, she leaped out again. "Obadiah! Over here! Over here!"

She held out an open book and watched the jellyhopper slide over the picture of a panda bear. Then she held out a sheet of blank paper. "Slide over this."

The panda bear appeared on the sheet of paper. It shone red, the same as the strange diagrams had done. "You are a photocopier. That's what you are. A living photocopier."

It had taken a long time to get to sleep with so much happening in her mind, but Isobel was up early, and now she wanted only to go off by herself and do some more thinking. She needed to decide whether to discuss her strange, new discovery with the children she had met the day before, or whether to say nothing.

After her father had left for work, Isobel raced to her room, pushed Obadiah into the backpack, and ran downstairs. "I'm playing down at the back of the yard," she called to Mrs. Hopgood.

"OK."

Isobel slipped into the old shed and was about to take Obadiah out of the pack when there was a tap on the door. She held the flap firmly shut. "Mrs. Hopgood?" queried Isobel, feeling both puzzled and surprised.

The door pushed open, but Mrs. Hopgood wasn't the person who opened it. Standing in front of Isobel was the girl called Ruth. "Hi. Um... Listen, Jamie sent me to tell you there's a meeting at ten o'clock in the barn."

Isobel stared. "A meeting? What do you mean, a meeting?"

Ruth's eyes flickered away a moment. She was embarrassed. "It's just the way he is. He likes to make things sound sort of important. He really means that he wants you to come and talk with us. No one else will be there."

Isobel kept staring at Ruth. "I don't know if that's a good idea. First of all, he's so bossy."

Ruth, whose embarrassment had been replaced by an air of friendliness, looked suddenly serious. "It's all right. He just gets bossy when he's surprised. You gave us a fright yesterday. We thought the bouncers had gotten away. And we haven't told anyone about them, and we didn't know if we really should have. And then finding you had one, too..." She looked away and then looked back, her eyes warm again. "I'd like you to come."

A small bubble of happiness floated suddenly and unexpectedly upward somewhere inside Isobel's chest. "All right, then," she said shyly. "I'll come."

Ruth clasped her hands as though she had just been given an exciting present. "Great! I'll go and tell Mrs. Hopgood that you're coming to play with us. So you'll be allowed. She knows my mother, you see. See you at ten o'clock."

The shed door shut behind her, and Isobel sat down on the box in the corner. Did the whole town know her business? She hadn't even known the three children existed; yet they knew where she lived, and even who looked after her for part of the day. She wondered what else they knew about her.

"Well, they don't know everything, do they?" she said, letting Obadiah slip out of the backpack. "They didn't know about you. And I bet they don't know everything you can do!"

Chapter 7

Ruth met Isobel as she crossed the field. She led her to Jamie and Reuben sitting in the dappled shade of an elderberry tree that grew close to the side of the old barn. Isobel felt suddenly shy, but trusting Ruth's friendliness, she was no longer frightened of the group.

Obadiah had begun humming as they crossed the field, and she lowered the backpack now and let him out. "I'll just let him in – to be with the others."

"Reuben," said Jamie, "you open the door just a tiny bit, enough for that bouncer to get through."

"I could have done it myself," Isobel said, with slight defiance, but she let Reuben do it and watched Obadiah slip through the gap. The humming in the barn was loud. Isobel grinned at Ruth. "Wow, it sounds like nine hundred jellyhoppers, not just nine."

Ruth smiled back. "I've never heard them so loud. We call them bouncers. But I think jellyhoppers sounds better. They are sort of like jelly."

"We're supposed to be having a meeting," Jamie called. Isobel wanted to tell him not to be so bossy, but Ruth made a face and rolled her eyes as though Jamie's bossiness was a joke. So Isobel grinned, instead, and followed Ruth to sit down on the grass near Jamie.

Reuben, who hadn't said a word since she arrived, looked suddenly at Isobel with laughing eyes. His hands were over his mouth as if they might be able to stop the laughter coming out. "Knock-knock," he managed to say.

Ruth replied before Isobel realized what he expected. "Who's there?" she said in a tired voice.

Reuben could hardly contain himself. "Isobel."

"Isobel who?" asked Ruth.

"Isobel necessary on a bicycle?" Reuben fell down laughing, while Isobel screwed up her nose at him. How was it that he knew her name? She hadn't told any of them.

"Reuben, shut up," said Jamie. "This is a meeting."

"We don't have to be so – so organized,"

protested Ruth. "We can just talk."

Reuben's face had gone solemn again. "I still think we should tell." He looked at Isobel. "Don't you think we should tell our parents?"

"Reuben, shut up." Jamie frowned. He looked at Isobel. "I'm Jamie Anderson, Ruth and Reuben's cousin. I'm staying with them while Mom and Dad are in Scandinavia. I'm twelve, so I'm in charge of this meeting. Ruth and Reuben's last name is Newton. Their house is over there." His arm waved vaguely in the direction of a house over the valley. The house was enclosed by trees, and only the gray tiles of part of the roof were visible.

"We know who you are because Mrs. Hopgood lives near us and knows Mom – and because Ribbonwood is small, it doesn't take long for the news to travel." Ruth was obviously going to say more, but Jamie spoke again.

"We thought we were the only ones who had found bouncers, and we believed that they came from the UFO that was seen on Friday night. Is that what you think about yours?"

"Yes," said Isobel, staring at Jamie's long, lean face, with its gray eyes and too-long fair hair. "I do."

The seriousness of Jamie's face seemed to relax a little. "We think that they are probably really important."

"They're the only space creatures I've ever heard of on Earth!" Ruth's face shone with excitement. "You haven't told anyone else about your creature, have you?"

"I still think we should tell our parents," Reuben broke in.

"Shut up, Reuben," said Jamie. He turned to Isobel. "Have you told anyone?"

"No."

Jamie allowed himself the tiniest smile of approval. "Good. We're making a detailed record of everything we know about them."

"You are," said Ruth.

Jamie opened a notebook that was resting on his lap. "We've written down everything about them that we know so far. Their size, shape, color – everything like that. Reuben is good at drawing, so he's done some illustrations, and I'm going to take some photos, but we wonder – "

"We wonder," said Ruth, "about getting photos developed. We wonder if the people who do it will want to know what they are. We haven't decided yet about telling anyone. Why didn't you tell anyone about the bouncer you found?"

Isobel didn't want to tell these children that she was lonely, that her secret had made her feel less lonely, that Obadiah was the only friend she had in this new town, and that looking after him, thinking and wondering about him, filled her day. Filled her days and her nights too well, she thought, thinking of the strange diagrams she had taken from her drawer that morning and put carefully into the pocket of the backpack.

But there was another reason that was just as important. "I didn't want Obadiah put in a cage.. You can't be sure, can you, what scientists might do with him."

In the short silence, Isobel knew they were all thinking of terrible experiments. Once she'd had nightmares for a whole week after she had watched half a television program about the way animals were used for testing products like shampoo. She pushed away the terrible pictures coming back into her mind. "They'd probably just look at him, at all of them, like we are. But you can't tell, can you?"

"That's what we're worried about, too," said Jamie. Isobel decided that, maybe, he might be quite nice after all.

"But what if they're dangerous?" said Reuben. "What if they give us a terrible disease? Or what if they take over the planet?"

"Reuben, don't be so dumb. How are eight – no, nine little animals going to take over a planet?" Ruth rolled her eyes again. "He watches

TV all the time and gets the dopiest ideas."

Jamie handed Isobel the notebook. She looked at the meticulously neat writing, with every heading carefully underlined, and decided Jamie must be very smart. There were words that she had never even heard of in the cleverly written sentences.

"What does "ovoid" mean?"

"Oval in shape," answered Jamie.

Isobel wondered why he didn't just say so. "They're flat on the bottom, though."

Under Jamie's heading "Initial Discovery," Isobel learned that the children had found the creatures at the edge of the potato crop when they, like Isobel and her father, had gone to the Richards' farm to investigate the strange story told by John Rogers. They had returned several times but found no more, so assumed, therefore, that there were no others.

There was a heading, "Sustenance," which Isobel guessed had something to do with food and surviving, because written underneath was the sentence "We have been unable to discover what the creatures eat, and it may be that they do not need to eat as we do. It may be that they draw sustenance from the air around us, or from some other process of which we have not yet become aware. As mentioned, there does not appear to be any form of mouth."

Reuben's drawings, which were very good, showed the wide, brown eyes and in one place had an arrow pointing to them, and a label – "Only visible facial organ."

Isobel looked up. "I know one thing they love to eat. Chocolate."

"Do they?" said Reuben disbelievingly.

"How can they?"

Jamie was looking at her keenly. How would he look, Isobel wondered, when she told him that Obadiah was a living machine? There was nothing in the notes that said he already knew that.

"Chocolate," said Jamie. "Is that how you got that bouncer to follow you?"

He certainly didn't miss much, thought Isobel. "Yes," she answered. She reached into her pocket and brought out the crumpled chocolate chip package that she had pilfered from the cupboard. "Come in the barn and I'll show you."

"We tried to get them to do things," said Ruth, "but they don't seem very intelligent in that sort of way." She giggled. "Perhaps we need to know another language for them to understand."

The initial excited humming had faded now from inside the barn. Reuben ran and pushed open the door. His voice reached the others before they saw what he was seeing. "WOW! Look at this! Hey, I told you they could take over. Hey! Look! Look at this!"

Chapter 8

The three other children crowded after Reuben.

"Watch it!" he complained indignantly, as they pushed past him. "I saw them first."

They all stood gazing at what Reuben had been yelling about. It was the number of jellyhoppers. They seemed to be everywhere. Obadiah still stood out as the largest one there, but there were very definitely more hoppers than there had been the day before.

"They've multiplied!" breathed Jamie.

"Multiplied?" Reuben sounded puzzled.

"How many are there?" asked Ruth. "They must breed faster than rabbits!"

"I thought you meant," said Reuben, "multiplied – like two times two is four, two times three is six..." The others ignored him.

"Perhaps they could take over." Ruth was staring at the creatures as if they might keep increasing before her eyes.

"Don't be stupid," snapped Jamie, and Isobel wondered if he was frightened by the thought. They were beautiful and quaint as pets. But were they pets? Were they animals?

"Machines," she murmured. "Taken over by machines."

"They're all crowding around Isobel," cried Reuben.

"It's the chocolate. They love chocolate. Try counting them, Jamie." Isobel walked slowly around the barn, holding the chocolate chip package in her hand. "I know they haven't got noses, but somehow they smell it."

It took some time, especially with Reuben insisting there were dozens, to discover that the number of jellyhoppers was exactly double what it had been.

"Exactly double," Jamie kept musing. "Exactly double our number of hoppers..."

"Isobel's one is the odd one out," said Ruth. "Hey, why did you call him Obadiah?"

"It fit," answered Isobel.

"Yes," agreed Ruth. "Yes, it does."

"They're even the same color," said Jamie. "Exactly double the number, and the same colors.

I'm wondering if they increase like amoebas."

"What's a memba?" asked Reuben.

"An amoeba," mouthed Jamie carefully. "A one-celled animal that reproduces by dividing in two."

"Oh... right..." said Reuben, obviously not really understanding.

"Come outside," said Jamie. "Shut them in and come outside."

"Here, Reuben," said Isobel. "You give them some chocolate – over there, and then run out the door."

"They'd go crazy in Mrs. Wynard's shop, wouldn't they, Ruth?" said Reuben, delighted to find the hoppers following him to the far corner of the barn.

The sunlight was bright outside. "Who's Mrs. Wynard?" asked Isobel.

"She has a little shop on the main street where she sells homemade chocolate. They cost the earth, but they are really yummy. Every two weeks or so she has this chocolate-making session. The smell is absolutely amazing. At this time of year, when the weather is hot and still, you can even smell it over here sometimes."

When Reuben was outside, Jamie drew a diagram of an amoeba in the back of his book of hopper notes. "Of course, being creatures of only one cell, amoebas are really tiny. But that's how they multiply, see. By dividing in half – it's called mitosis. I wonder if the jellyhoppers do the same thing."

"Then why hasn't Obadiah?" asked Ruth.

"Perhaps he's the father," suggested Reuben. "You know how things need a father..."

"Amoebas don't. That's the whole point. They just divide in half themselves," said Jamie. "But if that's what the hoppers do, and they keep doing it – "

"Tomorrow there could be thirty-two," said Ruth. "And after that, sixty-four. And then... And then, more than a hundred."

"One hundred and twenty-eight," said Isobel. She was good at math.

"We should really tell someone," said Reuben. "What are we going to do when they won't all fit in the barn?"

Isobel had a picture of the barn filled wall to wall with a mass of glowing red, yellow, and green jellyhoppers. "They'd look beautiful," she murmured.

Then, glancing up at Jamie's face, she saw that he looked worried. She thought again of what she had discovered about Obadiah last night.

"I don't really want to tell anyone about them," said Isobel. "It doesn't seem sort of right somehow." Ruth nodded, and Isobel knew she understood what she was saying, that they had made this stupendous discovery, and if they told parents and other adults about it, the jellyhoppers wouldn't be theirs anymore. They would become something quite different from the glowing, hopping, large-eyed creatures that loved chocolate.

But Isobel knew that they were already becoming something different than that for Jamie. She was trying not to let them change in her mind. She wanted Obadiah to stay a warm and comforting pet, but after last night, she couldn't help seeing him differently. She guessed that because Jamie felt himself to be in charge, he must feel even more responsible than any of them about what might be the right thing to do.

"Maybe before we really decide, you should know what else I found out about Obadiah."

"What?" said Jamie, leaning forward, almost indignantly. "What did you find out?"

Isobel took the few steps to her backpack, drew out the folded papers in the side pocket, and flattened them out. Ruth, Jamie, and Reuben peered at the odd, gleaming diagram on the top sheet.

"Obadiah made it. And these others. He did it like a photocopier does on an empty sheet of paper. I think he's some sort of living machine. Maybe they're all living machines."

Chapter 9

Isobel wasn't surprised that her father thought it was odd that she was heading off to bed early that night. She had a sense of surprise about it herself. But she needed to lie in bed and think awhile before she slept, go over the whole day, let the newness of everything become older and more comfortable because it had been turned over several times in her mind.

"Margery says the Newtons are a nice family," her father had smiled over dinner. "It's good that you've found some friends. The girl is your age, isn't she?"

"Three months older," replied Isobel.

She and Ruth had discovered that late in the afternoon when, with all the jellyhoppers except Obadiah locked safely in the barn, they went to

Isobel's house. Isobel had shown Ruth the sheds at the back of the yard, and the old trees. They had explored the house, and then sat on Isobel's bed, discussing things about each other that they had not had time to discuss during the excitement of the day.

There were short moments of shyness between them every now and then, but most of the time they had talked rapidly, each delighting in learning about the other. They were practically the same age. They both loved dogs and other animals. Isobel liked math, but Ruth preferred English. Both of their fathers were gloomy at breakfast time. Neither of them liked eating poached eggs, tapioca pudding, broccoli, or oysters. They both agreed on their favorite food: ice cream.

They discussed what they might be when they grew up, compared the worst and best teachers they had ever had, and decided which was their favorite of all TV programs they had ever watched.

Ruth had always lived in Ribbonwood. Isobel held back from telling her how she found moving so difficult, how lonely it could be in a new school. She needed to know that Ruth wanted to be friends as much as she did before she showed everything inside her head. For the same reason,

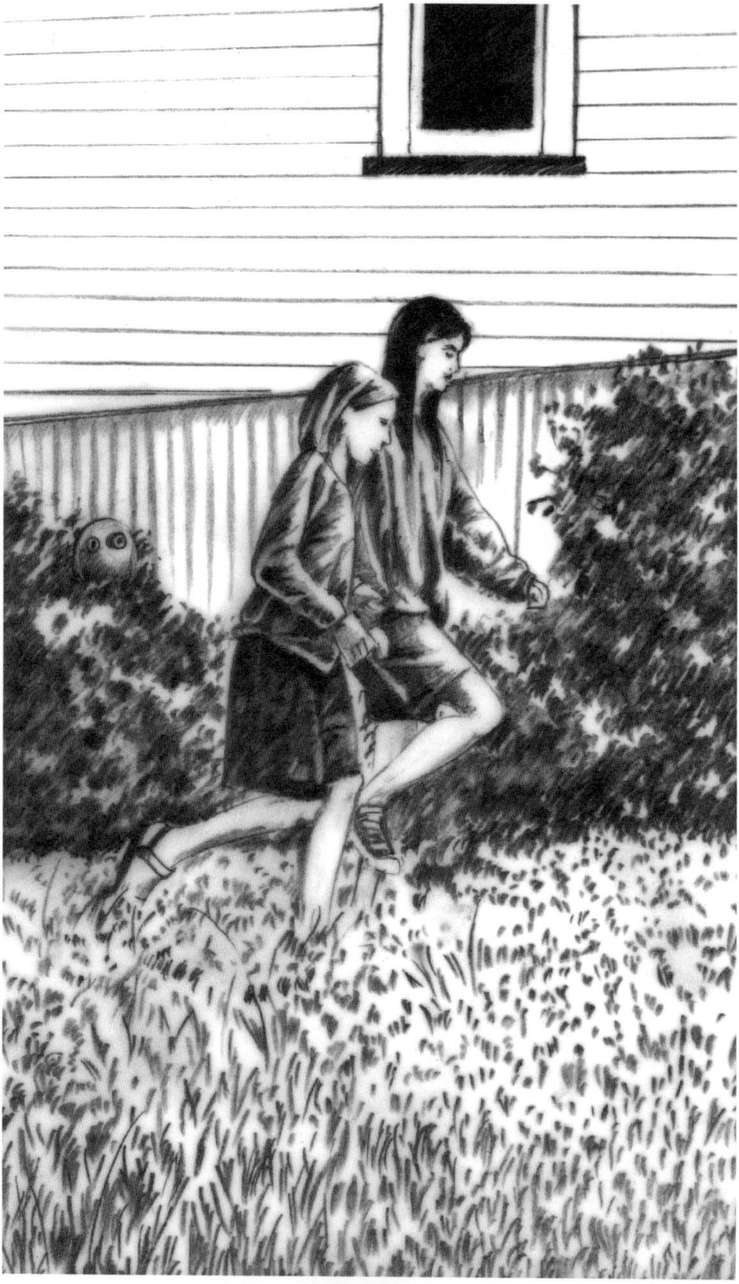

she didn't talk very much about her mother, who had died in a car crash so many years ago that Isobel couldn't remember her, even when she tried most desperately. Ruth's mother worked in the school office and, therefore, was home during vacations. Isobel wondered what she was like.

It was interesting to Isobel, an only child, that Reuben looked so much like Ruth. She wondered if it felt something like having a shadow, having a person look so similar. Ruth said that Reuben wouldn't tell anyone about the jellyhoppers if they told him not to. Isobel wasn't so sure that a kid of eight could be trusted. He seemed so worried by their secret.

Isobel frowned, remembering for a moment Reuben's silly joke; and then she smiled, recalling that catching some terrible interplanetary disease was one of his fears. Machines didn't get diseases.

At least that's what she'd thought, until Jamie had gone on about computer viruses. She hadn't understood, except to realize whatever he was talking about transferred from one machine to another, not to people. Jamie knew a lot about computers – partly because his parents had some sort of business involving them. Isobel didn't understand that either, except for the fact that their overseas trip was related to their work.

Jamie knew a lot about everything, and Isobel decided that knowing so much was partly why Jamie got so worried about things. He knew more things to worry about.

He had been terribly excited by Isobel's discovery of Obadiah's photocopying abilities. His hands had trembled with excitement as he looked at the strange diagrams Isobel handed him.

"Don't you see?" Isobel could still hear him saying the words. "Don't you see? These are – these are absolutely unique! They must have been stored inside him until he went over the paper. We are holding diagrams from another planet! Diagrams made by someone from another planet!"

Isobel was a little puzzled by his excitement. Weren't creatures from another planet every bit as exciting? Maybe he had been this way when he first found the hoppers.

"Is it a message?" Reuben's voice had sounded wary, as if the diagrams may be news of a coming horror.

Jamie had looked at the diagrams for a long time, turning them this way and that, comparing one with another, trying his best to make some sense from the symbols, trying to understand what the purpose of each total diagram might be.

Isobel and Ruth were at first engrossed by his excitement, by his mutterings and sudden exclamations; and then they speculated between themselves about a variety of possibilities.

"They could be diagrams about terrible weapons," said Ruth, who, like Isobel, felt slightly nervous about aliens from another planet.

"Or, they could be," said Isobel, putting on an immensely serious expression so that Ruth waited goggle-eyed for her thoughts, "the plans for building a fast-food chain on all the planets." They rolled on the grass laughing and felt their nervousness disappear.

None of the three noticed that Reuben had collected some of the blank sheets of paper by Isobel's pack and slipped into the barn. They saw him only when he returned, dangling the sheets of paper by one corner as though he shouldn't touch them more than was necessary.

"Some of the other ones do it, too. They do the copying. Not all of them. But some do."

Isobel had felt sorry for Jamie. It seemed that while he was the smartest of all of them, it was everyone else who made the major discoveries.

They had all been late for lunch while they tried to decide which of the hoppers still had stored information. It was very difficult.

They took more paper back to the barn after lunch. Isobel's father, after his midday phone call to Mrs. Hopgood, was happy to let Isobel spend the afternoon with the Newton children. Jamie had cleverly arrived with some chocolate. At least they had one way of keeping some hoppers at one end of the barn while they encouraged others to slide over blank sheets.

"It must be the first ones we found that have the information stored," said Jamie.

"If they divided in half, without a father or anything," said Reuben, "the information could have divided in half, too." He had become happily involved with the whole experiment and seemed no longer afraid of the peculiar diagrams, or the unusual spirals of symbols that had appeared on three sheets.

It was when Jamie had sat down with his book to record this new and amazing development that Ruth and Isobel had gone off to Isobel's house.

"You could help," grumbled Jamie.

"You're far better at it than we are," said Ruth. "We'll have a look at it later."

"I'll help," Reuben offered eagerly. "And when you've finished, we can put it under one of the hoppers and get a copy! So if your book gets stolen or anything, well, we've still got the information."

Jamie had looked at Reuben with a new respect. "Yes. We could."

Isobel and Ruth were heading out the door.

"Hey – Isobel," called Jamie. "You're taking

Obadiah, aren't you? See if you can keep him hidden at your place for a day or two – just in case he does have anything to do with the others multiplying. We'll see what happens when he isn't here."

His face had the worried look again, and Ruth couldn't help giggling. "Poor Jamie. He doesn't know what to think about first."

"I don't think I do either," said Isobel.

"Let's not think about any of it for awhile. Put Obadiah in your pack, and we'll go to your place and just think about us. What's your favorite color? Mine's blue. Blue like the sky is now."

Isobel snuggled down in her bed, remembering. She closed her eyes and let the blue of a summer sky fill every space in her head until she felt as though she was floating. Floating in blueness... that changed to the purple of dusk light... and deepened into almost black, in which glowing green and red and yellow creatures floated with her... and they floated, she and the glowing creatures – and Ruth was with them, too, in and out of shapes drawn in shining red on the blackness...

Morning St

Established 1919

UFO SIGHTING DISCREDITED

RIBBONWOOD. The "spacecraft" sighted by two Ribbonwood residents on July 5 was probably a meteorite," stated Dr. Stanley Chang, an Arawera Research Station scientist investigating the claim.

Meteorites are fragments of rock or metal from outer space, and are of sufficient size to survive their fiery passage to Earth. Dr. Chang said it was likely that the "smoking heaps of metal" which farm worker John Rogers claimed to have seen on the ground were, in fact, the remains of the meteorite burning out.

According to Dr. Chang, "This unusual phenomenon would explain Rogers' sighting of an object in the sky, as well as the burned area in the potato crop."

Soil in the immediate area is being tested to confirm this theory, which is supported by air traffic control. However, a leading international UFO proponent, Mr. Aidan Petrosky, disputed the Arawera research team findings.

"The two witnesses are both respected members of the local community," he said, after flying from Washington, D.C. to investigate the Richards' property in Ribbonwood. "They both know what they saw, and I believe them." **cont. page E2**

Chapter 10

"Sounds much more probable to me." Mr. Miro was mumbling and nodding as he read the morning paper.

Isobel, peering over his shoulder, knew he was talking about the possibility of the meteorite. Of course, she didn't agree with that idea, but she didn't say anything. It was better that people didn't believe in the possibility of a spacecraft visitation, for then it seemed more likely that the secret of the jellyhoppers could be kept. Of course, if by accident any of the jellyhoppers were seen, people wouldn't have to believe in spacecrafts to think the creatures were very definitely odd and unusual and worth investigating.

Before her father left for work, the telephone rang. "It's for you, Izzy," called Mr. Miro, and

Isobel felt a start of surprise.

Ruth spoke to her. "Mom is taking us – because Jamie's here just now – to visit some of our other cousins. It takes nearly two hours to get there and I hate going, but it's all right when we're there. Except I wish we weren't going at all because we'll be away all day, and we won't be able to go to the barn." Ruth's voice had become almost a whisper. "Can you go and check – just make sure everything's OK?" Her voice became normal again. "Mom says that next time we're going somewhere for the day, you can come if you like."

Isobel felt herself blushing with pleasure, but at the same time, she felt disappointment that she wouldn't be able to share her day with the children. "I'll check. Tell Jamie not to worry."

"Here's Reuben," said Ruth's voice.

"Isobel," said Reuben. "Would you check my guinea pig?"

"Guinea pig? Check it for what? I don't even know where it is."

Isobel heard Reuben's voice complaining, "She doesn't know where it is."

Ruth was back on the phone. "Honestly! His stupid guinea pig will be fine, but it got its leg caught in the cage wire the other day and Reuben is convinced it could die if someone doesn't check up on it. It won't, of course, but do you mind?"

72

"I don't mind, but I've never been to your house," Isobel said.

"You know where it is," Ruth said. "Just go across the field and through the gate at the back. The cage is on the lawn at the end of the house. Just have a look in it."

When Isobel's father knew that she wasn't spending time with the children, he mentioned it to Mrs. Hopgood.

"That's no problem at all. I have a friend visiting this afternoon. She has a girl about Isobel's age, and I was going to ask if she'd come and play with her. So that's just fine."

Isobel knew it was no use protesting. Earlier in the vacation, she had spent several uninspiring afternoons at Mrs. Hopgood's. Maybe someone else there might make it slightly more interesting. She just hoped Mrs. Morrow and Angela weren't the people visiting.

"I'm very glad you're getting to know lots of other children," said Mr. Miro, as he thrust some papers into his briefcase. "I'm getting to know lots of people, too."

Isobel thought that was an odd thing to say. Of course, he would be getting to know lots of people – all the people that worked in the bank, all the customers who came in and out, and all the people in the stores nearby.

"I'm going out with one of them tonight. Sue Akers. You met Sue, Isobel, at the Morrow's." Her father was unusually bright this morning.

"Yes," said Isobel.

"And my neighbor's daughter is going to baby-sit," said Mrs. Hopgood. "I'm busy tonight."

Isobel felt a small surge of irritation at the way her life was being organized. "Why do you have to go out, anyway?" she said to her father, ignoring Mrs. Hopgood.

"There's a good movie, and this is the last night it's on. Have a nice day and be good."

People might be able to organize parts of my life, thought Isobel, but they don't know my secret. They don't know our secret. She blotted out her irritation with a picture of herself, Jamie, Ruth, and Reuben surrounded by jellyhoppers in a photo on the front page of the *Morning Star*. Underneath she put a headline: "Ribbonwood Children World Famous."

Later in the morning, she told Mrs. Hopgood that she was going to check Reuben's guinea pig, explaining about its leg.

"I could have checked it myself," said Mrs. Hopgood, "if I'd known. But the walk will do you good. Goodness! For a moment I thought that backpack of yours moved! You don't secretly keep a snake in there, do you?"

Mrs. Hopgood laughed at her joke, and Isobel hastily jiggled the pack. "No, no snakes."

She realized Mrs. Hopgood was wondering why she wore a backpack at all. "I've got some... um... paper in here. I like to draw sometimes – down in the big shed."

"That shed's like having your own special playhouse, isn't it," smiled Mrs. Hopgood. "Have you made your bed?"

Isobel assured Mrs. Hopgood that her work was done, picked up a pen next to the telephone to further emphasize her interest in drawing, and went.

She didn't let Obadiah out of her backpack until she was nearly at the Newtons' house, afraid that he might detour to the barn. "Come on, Obadiah. You are going to visit a guinea pig."

The back gate was hinged to a large tree, and although Isobel felt kind of like an intruder, she was intrigued by the short, woodland path that led to the well-ordered yard around the house. At first she couldn't find any sign of a cage alongside the house. Then, across the rose beds, she spotted one and headed toward it.

Obadiah took no interest in the animal. Nor did the guinea pig appear to notice the jellyhopper. "You could have been good friends, you two," Isobel rebuked them.

Reuben's pet looked perfectly healthy, as Ruth had said it would. Isobel looked up and couldn't help noticing through some French doors that the room on the end of the house was obviously Ruth's. As Ruth had envied Isobel's upstairs bedroom, Isobel envied Ruth's with its doors that opened straight into the yard. She sat down on the grass, drew a sheet of paper and the pen out of her backpack, and wrote in large letters:

SEE YOU TOMORROW.
GUINEA PIG IS FINE!
– ISOBEL

Scooping up Obadiah from near the rose bed, she put him down in front of the sheet and watched him slide over it. Then she put a blank sheet of paper in front of him and watched as her words appeared again in glowing red when Obadiah slid over that piece. She had him copy the words three more times, then rolled the five sheets of paper together and labeled the outside: **MESSAGE FROM A FRIEND**. Writing the words gave her great satisfaction. She tucked the roll in behind the handle of the French doors.

"Come on, Obadiah." She headed back around the house, down the short woodland path, and out into the field, her strange green companion hopping along behind her. She thought she must have

Jamie write in his book that the creatures (or were they machines?) were trainable. She knew Obadiah followed her only in the hope of getting some chocolate, but at least he *was* following her.

Then, suddenly, he wasn't following her. He was leaping ahead, humming a little, excited that he was near the barn and the other hoppers. Isobel, aware of Jamie's instructions to keep Obadiah away from the other hoppers, raced after him and caught up just before he reached the barn.

Chapter 11

Isobel peeked in the barn door. There were jellyhoppers everywhere – many more than there had been yesterday. If they had doubled again, as she had guessed they might, there would now be thirty-two of them.

Thirty-two jellyhoppers! And to think that only a few days ago she had thought Obadiah was the only space creature on Earth!

Isobel sat outside the barn for awhile, until Obadiah's wriggling and humming in the backpack became too much. "All right. Let's go."

She had done as Jamie instructed and kept Obadiah away from the others. Would that mean that tomorrow the number would still be thirty-two, or would it have made no difference? Would there then be sixty-four? Sixty-four!

She wondered again, as she crossed the field, whether the creatures had any other special abilities she and the other children had not yet discovered. She wondered whether the jellyhoppers would keep multiplying until there were thousands and thousands and millions of them. If they did, and they were like a plague on the earth, would the world find out that it was she and Jamie and Ruth and Reuben who had allowed them to multiply before the scientists had known of their existence, and would they be punished?

She wondered whether the people from the other planet knew the creatures were here. Had they let them come deliberately? Or had they fallen accidentally from the troubled spacecraft? What were the strange diagrams and the spirals of symbols? Special messages, or simply space-office photocopying? The small pricklings of fear, slight but real, rippled uncomfortably down Isobel's back as she thought of aliens and messages and other worlds. Perhaps she should have told about Obadiah the minute she found him. Perhaps the others should have told about their find, too.

She let Obadiah out in the shed, took out some paper, and wrote the question WHAT SHALL WE DO? She had Obadiah copy it twice on other sheets of paper.

"I'm going to write down all the – what do you

call it? All the – all the options. Ready to discuss tomorrow." She looked at Obadiah, and ran a hand over his warm, green body. "I don't think you're really a machine. You're a special kind of animal. If I kept you, you could be so handy at school. I could write things down, and the whole class could have their work copied into their book without having to lift a pen. You know, that's what you could be wherever you come from – a schoolchild's photocopier. Those diagrams could be their math or science. I'm sure you are quite harmless."

She wondered if she and Ruth would be in the same room when school started. She dreamed about it for awhile – then began her list.

In the afternoon, when she had to go with Mrs. Hopgood, she left Obadiah shut in the shed. Alice, the girl that she played with, didn't come from Ribbonwood. She was vacationing with Mrs. Hopgood's friend. Isobel knew she would probably never see her again. She wasn't as special as Ruth, but she was nice, and Isobel wouldn't have minded getting to know her some more.

The neighbor's daughter who came to baby-sit that evening, while her father went out with Sue, wasn't nearly as interesting. Her name was Lisa. She had long hair that kept falling over her eyes so that she had to push it back from her face every minute or two. She didn't want to play any board games. She didn't want to explore outside. (Isobel didn't want to either, as there was a gusty wind blowing.) She didn't want to look at Isobel's room or any of her possessions. She didn't want to talk. She just wanted to watch television, and she looked at Isobel as if she was a pest who had to be put up with.

Isobel went off to her bedroom early. She let Obadiah hop up the stairs – knowing that Lisa wouldn't know what was happening anywhere except on the TV screen. "At least Ruth and the others will be home tomorrow," Isobel told him. "We'll have to decide about you and all your jellyhopper friends, I suppose." She knew Jamie would be very concerned when he saw there were thirty-two of them. And quite beside himself if there were sixty-four!

Isobel thought of calling the Newtons' house, but apart from feeling suddenly shy – for she had seldom called friends – she knew they might be late getting home. She read for a long time, and then fell sound asleep in spite of the gusting wind. She didn't hear her father come home, or Lisa go. She didn't hear anything until one o'clock in the morning – and it was Obadiah who woke her.

Isobel had never before seen him jumping around the edges of the room as if he was looking for a way to escape. His humming came in short, high bursts, very loudly.

"Shhhh, Obadiah," moaned Isobel. "You'll wake up Dad."

The humming continued, and, as Isobel became fully awake, she climbed out of bed, took hold of the jellyhopper, and thrust him in bed under the sheet. He had been content there other times; but this time, before Isobel herself had climbed back in, Obadiah was out, hopping around the room and humming loudly.

"You'll wake Dad!" Even as she said it, she knew it was no use. He couldn't understand.

"You're a pest," she hissed angrily, worried that the noise would bring her father in to investigate. She dragged a sweatshirt on over her nightgown, and slipped sandals on her feet. Then she picked up the backpack and thrust Obadiah inside. He leaped out before she could shut the flap. Greatly surprised, Isobel grabbed him again and thrust him back.

She slipped out the door and down the stairs. Her eyes were accustomed now to the dark, and she didn't turn on any lights. It was very quiet in the house, for the gusty wind had dropped. The creaking of the stairs seemed loud.

Isobel wished she could put Obadiah in the cupboard underneath them, but he would still be heard there. She was going to have to take him outside and lock him in the shed. And she didn't much like being out in the dark on her own.

She unlocked the back door, and slipped outside. "Shhhh, Obadiah!" The world outside was warm and very still. Isobel looked up at the starry sky with its small crescent moon. It was wide and beautiful. Isobel looked down. The shadows of tree and building looked as if they might leap at her. Obadiah was still humming and wriggling.

Isobel took a deep breath and ran, as fast as she could, down the yard to the old sheds. As she went, she could smell an amazing smell. Chocolate! Mrs. Wynard must have made chocolates today and, as the children had said it did, the smell was drifting on the still air. Isobel half-wondered if that was what had excited Obadiah.

Her racing feet stopped outside the shed. She hated opening the door, knowing the blackness that would be on the other side. She knelt to open the backpack first.

And Obadiah was off! Jumping out into the field, glowing in an almost luminous way in the night dimness.

"Oh, no!" cried Isobel, forgetting her fear of the dark as she whirled around to chase after him. She stopped. There, out in the field, like a billowing, glittering length of cloth in red and yellow and green, were all the jellyhoppers from the barn, hopping and glowing and progressing across the field in a direction that would take them closest to the town center. Obadiah was going to join them, and the smell of chocolate hung heavy in the air.

Chapter 12

"They're going to town! They're all going into town!"

Isobel didn't stop to wonder how they had gotten out of the barn. Her feet were as fast as running water as she raced across the field in the other direction. Running, running, running until she reached the back gate leading into the Newtons' house.

Stopping for breath, she leaned on the gate and suddenly saw the shadows of the woodland path. But she couldn't stop now. She concentrated hard on thoughts of daytime and sunshine and flowers, and she ran through the trees so quickly that she felt surprise when she was suddenly on the lawn. She crept then, quietly, trying to keep her breath from being so noisy, around the house to the French doors of the room that she knew was Ruth's.

"Please don't let anyone see me. Please don't let anyone hear me. No one but Ruth," she whispered between her panting breaths.

She hesitated a moment, then tapped on the French doors. "Ruth. It's me, Isobel. Don't be scared. Ruth. It's me, Isobel. Ruth, it's Isobel."

She stopped a moment, listened, then tapped again, calling in a loud whisper over and over. "Ruth, it's just me. It's Isobel. Open the door."

Her heart was pounding, and she leaped with fright when the curtains moved suddenly in front of her face. But it was Ruth's face, peering cautiously through the glass. The door opened, and Isobel spoke before Ruth could.

"It's the jellyhoppers! They're all out! They're going into town. And there're thirty-two of them now!"

"What? Thirty-two! To town! Isobel – "

"Quick. Get Jamie!"

Ruth seemed suddenly to become fully awake. She pulled on shorts and a shirt. Isobel, waiting, felt sudden terror that Mr. or Mrs. Newton may suddenly appear from another doorway of the house and demand to know what she, a stranger, was doing in Ruth's bedroom in the middle of the night.

Ruth slipped out her bedroom door. Isobel tried to look like part of the doorframe as she shrank against it, waiting. Then she could hear

Ruth and Jamie coming. Surely Mr. and Mrs. Newton would wake up!

Jamie was in shorts and T-shirt, as though it were really daytime, but his hair, unbrushed, was sticking out at odd angles. He blinked a lot. "How do you know – " he began in a stern whisper.

Isobel couldn't believe that he was going to put on a bossy act now, when at any moment Ruth's parents could appear, when all thirty-two jellyhoppers – thirty-three counting Obadiah – had escaped and were heading into town.

"I know because I saw them!" she hissed angrily at him. "Now, come on!"

She was out through the French doors and around the corner of the house, hardly looking behind to check that Jamie and Ruth were following. She knew they would be.

The shadows on the woodland path didn't matter now. In fact, suddenly, as the soft grass of the field beyond swished about her feet, it was a great and glorious thing to be out in the night. The Newtons hadn't woken to question what was going on, and now that Jamie and Ruth were with her, the situation wasn't as scary. She looked again at the wide night sky spread with stars, and she wished that she was out here with her friends only for the joy of being out.

"Jamie, there are thirty-two jellyhoppers now,

plus Obadiah, and they are all out! I think it's the chocolate smell. I think they're looking for the chocolate in town. Do you know the quickest way to get there?"

Ruth was beside her. "But how are we going to stop them?"

Isobel stopped for a second. "I don't know. I don't know!" She turned to Jamie. "How can we stop them?"

"Are you sure you saw them? I can't see them," he persisted.

"I saw them all right! I saw them." Isobel followed now behind Jamie and Ruth. "They looked amazing. A great, long, colored – well, it was sort of like a wide, wavy ribbon – a glittering ribbon of jellyhoppers."

"I still can't see them," said Jamie, and his voice suggested he didn't want to – so that Isobel would be proved wrong.

"It's the chocolate. They're heading for the chocolate," said Ruth.

"I'm glad someone believes me," said Isobel.

"Of course we believe you," said Ruth. "Don't we, Jamie?"

Jamie made a small noise that could have been a yes or could have been a no. Then he said bossily, "Stay close together and don't talk. And can't you walk a bit more softly, Ruth?"

They were hurrying through the Ribbonwood streets, into the shopping area. Isobel wished again they could be out on this night walk just for the joy of it, for it was exciting now, with company, to be hurrying through the light and shadow of the world by night. No other person shared this world with them, only a prowling black cat that could easily have been mistaken for a shadow. The mannequins in the window of Ribbonwood's only small department store still smiled. On a small, make-believe beach created in the pharmacist's window, sunglasses and suntan lotion advertised themselves by moonlight.

"Reuben will be mad he's not here," said Isobel. "Are we nearly at the store? If the hoppers aren't there, what will we do? Where else do you think they might have gone?"

"I'd like to know how they got out," said Ruth.

"Shhhhh!" hissed Jamie.

But it was Jamie who, in the next minute, cried out. As they turned the corner into the small side street where Mrs. Wynard's chocolate shop was, two men nearly collided with the three children. The men were running fast.

The men's eyes showed a small, sudden start of surprise at the sight of the three children, but they didn't stop running, and the children didn't turn to watch where they went because a third man, clad in dark clothes like the other two, was disappearing into the door of Mrs. Wynard's chocolate shop. They all heard him muttering in panic-stricken tones, "I have to get the stupid thing."

After the quietness of the deserted streets, the unexpected burst of action was so sudden it was frightening. While the two girls stared, open-mouthed, Jamie cried out, "It's open! The shop's open!" And what he was really saying was that there was something very wrong happening, and he didn't understand yet what it was.

Then the third man was flying out of the shop door again, looking even more frantic than the first two men, and stuffing a card into his pocket as he went.

Isobel recognized the look on the third man's face as the same that she had seen on other adults if she held out a frog for them to hold, or offered them a garden worm. "It's the jellyhoppers! They're inside!" She was first in the door, and Ruth and Jamie were close behind.

The smell of chocolate was almost sickening inside the shop. The three children's eyes took in the sight of the opened cash register, askew on the counter among the tall, glass jars of chocolates with mouth-watering names. Even as they realized that the three men had been robbing the shop, the

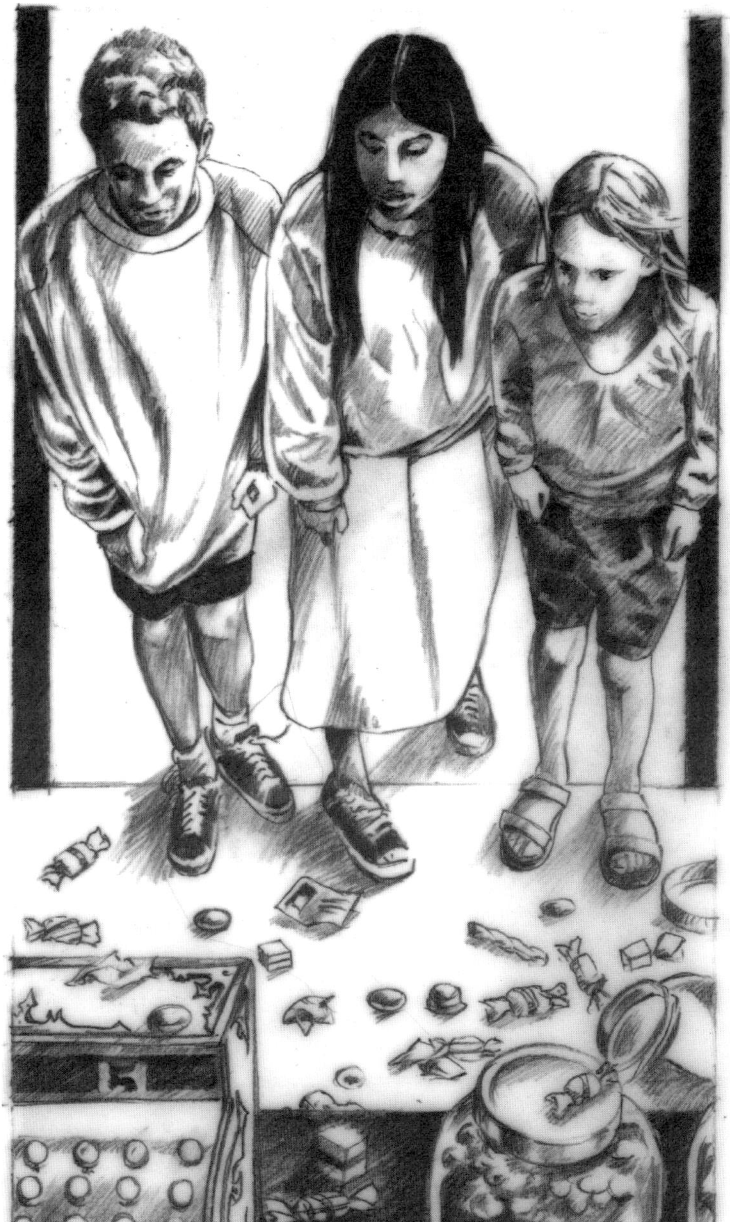

fact seemed unimportant. What did seem important was that the jellyhoppers, all thirty-three of them, were in the shop. They could see them, glimmering, in the back portion of the small building, through the beaded curtain that screened off the work area.

On a long trestle, Mrs. Wynard had left many trays of freshly made chocolates – chocolate in bars, chocolates in ruffled papers, chocolates in sets of metal molds, chocolate mice, and chocolate people resting on waxed paper. In the high ceiling above the trestle, a skylight was open. Just as the children had realized there had been a robbery, they realized also that it had been through this skylight that the smell of chocolate had drifted, and through this skylight that at least one of the men had climbed to gain entry to the shop.

The jellyhoppers couldn't have gotten through a skylight, but they hadn't needed to when the men had opened the door. They were feasting now on the rich spread of fresh chocolates, a humming host of hoppers, their glowing colors shimmering as they jumped and slid over and under each other. It was a truly amazing sight.

Chapter 13

"I never realized before," said Ruth as she stared at the sight, "that they don't blink. Their eyes move, but they don't have eyelids for blinking. Yet they have eyelashes. I wonder – "

"Stop carrying on, Ruth! We have to do something. And quickly! Really quickly!" Jamie was standing tense and still, except for his hands, which clenched and unclenched.

"I think the jellyhoppers scared the burglars," said Isobel.

"If I was a burglar and these guys walked in," said Ruth, nodding toward the hoppers, "I'd be surprised, too."

"We have to do something," Jamie repeated. He seemed, except for his hands, incapable of moving. "Unbelievable! Thirty-three of them!"

"I know!" cried Isobel suddenly. "I know what we can do!" She grabbed a large box standing against the wall and scooped up the chocolates on the trays. She picked up the metal molds and emptied the contents into the box. She tugged the waxed paper out from under the chocolate mice and the chocolate people, letting them fall in a tumble into the box.

"Come on! Help me! Get all the chocolate in the box, and then we can make them follow us!"

"That's right!" A delighted smile spread over Jamie's face, and he sprang into action. "They can't get the chocolate in the jars. We just have to get all the loose stuff. Come on, Ruth!"

The jellyhoppers, realizing their food was disappearing into the box, began jumping over it so that Jamie had to hold it up higher than the hoppers could jump. The girls scooped and snatched between the soft, warm creatures, crying "Down!" every time they wanted Jamie to lower the box to allow them to toss in more booty. They gathered every piece of freshly made chocolate that the jellyhoppers hadn't already eaten. Then Jamie tipped in the contents of two jars on the counter.

"Check that you can't see anyone on the street, Isobel," Jamie ordered. "Ruth, you'll have to help me with this box when we get outside. It's heavy."

"Let's not go back up the main street," said

Ruth. "Let's go on down this street and home the back way. It's probably safer."

No house lights shone from windows, only street lights here and there, as the strange procession wound its way along the sidewalk. Jamie and Ruth, holding the box, led the way, and Isobel followed behind the thirty-three jellyhoppers, which were eagerly pursuing the smell of fresh chocolate. She felt again the magic of night – and there was a special edge to the feeling, now that the jellyhoppers were in their control. Soon they would have them safely in the barn.

She let a small, singsong chant escape and repeat itself in the night as they moved down the silent streets. "There's no one else about. It's only us that's out. There's no one else about. It's only us that's out. There's no one else about. It's only –"

Suddenly, there *was* someone else – John Rogers, standing two feet from her on the sidewalk! John Rogers, witness to the spacecraft visit, standing and staring in amazement. He had emerged from the gateway of a small block of apartments, which were almost hidden by the high, wooden fence bordering the sidewalk. Isobel realized that he was probably heading for his car parked on the street. But he was so startled by the sight of three children and thirty-three jellyhoppers moving through the night that he stood, unable to move, his mouth open, his eyes blinking rapidly.

Isobel suddenly wanted to laugh. She leaned forward as she walked past him. "We're not really here, you know," she said in a ghostly voice. "It's all in your imagination."

She made herself keep walking at the same pace until the whole procession had rounded the corner, and then, giggling, she raced past the hoppers to Ruth and Jamie.

"John Rogers! We just passed John Rogers!" She waved an arm behind her. Jamie thrust the box suddenly at her so that she had to grasp it to save it from falling, and he ran back to the corner and peered around it.

He was back in a few seconds, grabbing the box back from Isobel. "He's standing there staring! Come on, before he wakes up again."

Isobel stayed at the front, and the three children ran through the streets. Ruth, panting, managed to explain, "His friend lives in an apartment on that street. He'll have been there."

"Don't talk!" Jamie hissed at them. "Come on – we've got to hurry."

Only at the edge of town did they let their feet slow to a walking pace; and Isobel, confused by the unknown streets, could see that they were at the corner of the field where the barn waited in the night for its escaped inmates. Jamie and

Ruth rested the carton on a fence post, and threw a handful of chocolate to the jellyhoppers.

Then, less hurriedly, they crossed the field and saw as they approached the barn that one of the doors swung wide, creaking now and then when a small, rising breeze moved it.

They never discovered whether the door had been opened by someone, whether Isobel hadn't latched it properly after her visit, or whether the excited jellyhoppers themselves had pushed and jumped against it until it gave way.

Inside the barn, the jellyhoppers hummed and clustered around the trail of chocolate that the children made on the floor. It was simple to shut the door securely, with all the creatures inside.

"We should've kept some!" cried Ruth suddenly. "Some of the chocolates. For the hoppers to eat later."

"Oh, yeah... We should have," agreed Isobel.

"No," said Jamie. "No. It's better if they're all gone. Then people won't know we took them – there'll be no evidence."

Ruth frowned. "You mean that people would think we stole them? We had to take them to get the jellyhoppers out."

"How can we explain that?" Jamie kicked morosely at a clump of grass. "And John Rogers saw us."

"He shouldn't have been out so late," said Ruth, her tone suddenly as gloomy as Jamie's. "I told Isobel he was probably visiting his friend. He should have been home by this hour of the night, not suddenly appearing on the street when people aren't expecting it."

Isobel giggled suddenly, and the other two glowered at her.

"What's funny about it?" asked Jamie.

"I told him we weren't there," chuckled Isobel. "That he was imagining it!"

Ruth began a slow grin. "Did he believe you?"

"I don't know," said Isobel, "but he looked so dazed about what he was seeing that he might have. He might really think he did imagine it."

"See, Jamie," said Ruth. "It'll be OK." She giggled, too. "Poor guy. The scientists are making him sound as though he imagined the spacecraft. He'll start to think he's really cracking up."

The girls could see Jamie's face relax a little. Then he frowned again. "Those men – "

"They won't say anything." Ruth laughed, remembering. "Can you imagine their faces when all the jellyhoppers came into the store?"

"I know they won't say anything about us," said Jamie. "In fact, I don't know if they even saw us, really. But we should be saying something about them. They were robbing the store."

There was a silence and each knew the other was trying to work out how they could say anything without revealing they had been at the store themselves.

Finally, Isobel said, "People will find out, anyway, that the store has been burglarized."

Ruth, ever hopeful, said, "Perhaps it hasn't been burglarized! Perhaps the jellyhoppers scared the men before they had taken any money!"

Isobel and Jamie didn't say anything.

"It's possible!" protested Ruth.

Of course it is," said Isobel.

"Let's go home and go to bed," said Jamie, "now that our crazy hoppers are all inside." He gave the barn door a kick. "We'll have to tell about them. We probably should have told in the first place."

orning Star

Established 1919   ★★★   **Volume LXXVI**

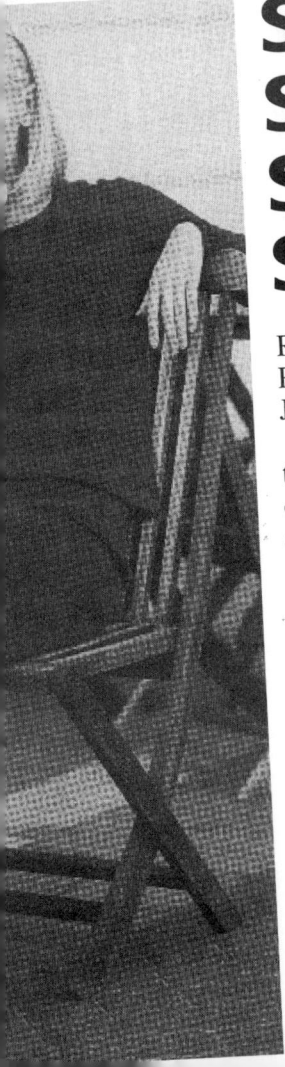

SPACECRAFT SPOTTER SUPPORTS SIGHTING

RIBBONWOOD. Ribbonwood farmhand John Rogers, the man who claimed he saw a UFO on July 5, remains steadfast in his original assertion.

But the Arawera research team investigating the alleged sighting has disputed the Rogers claim. They believe what he saw was, in fact, a meteorite.

Rogers was unavailable today for comment about the matter. His employer, Ribbonwood farmer Tom Richards, said that Rogers had decided to take a two-week vacation, as he felt he was being "bothered by the media over the incident" and needed to get away for some "time out."

"John remains adamant that what he saw was not a meteorite," said Mr. Richards. "He feels that the scientists' conclusion is making him look like a liar."

One other Ribbonwood resident has claimed to have seen the craft. Scientists are still investigating the matter, but it is believed that the inquiry will be brought to a close. **cont. page D3**

Chapter 14

Isobel's father woke her when he came to say good-bye before going to work. "Were up half the night, weren't you?" he asked, so that her eyes flew open in sudden alarm. Then she realized that he thought she had stayed up late with the sitter.

"I went to bed early," she protested.

For awhile after her father had gone, she lay in bed, half-asleep, turning over last night's events in her mind. The paper, she thought suddenly. There'll be something about the burglary.

She read some of the article about John Rogers. "He hasn't gone far away for his vacation," she snorted.

"I didn't think it said where he was," said Mrs. Hopgood.

"No. No, it doesn't. I made a mistake." Isobel

closed her mouth firmly, as Mrs. Hopgood carried on dusting. She looked carefully, she thought, through every column.

"The burglary was just a tiny paragraph, right on the bottom of the front page," Jamie told her later. "I suppose they didn't hear about it until the paper was nearly ready to print. It said further details will be published later."

"I still don't know what you all keep talking about," Reuben protested for the umpteenth time, his voice rising to a pitch of fury that Ruth recognized as dangerous. "You keep saying things that I don't know about and you make them sound important. And why are you talking about a burglary?"

"Come here, Reuben, I'll tell you all about it," said Ruth. "But you can't complain that you weren't there. We had to rush off, and we couldn't wait around to wake you up."

"Rush off where? What are you talking about?"

"Just listen!"

Jamie and Isobel left them to it and headed for the barn door. Jamie carried his camera. "I'm going to take some photos. If we're going to have to tell, we may as well at least have some photos for ourselves."

"Wonder if they've eaten all the chocolate," said Isobel. She didn't want to talk yet about having to tell about the jellyhoppers, although the prospect didn't seem as bad as it had just two days ago. In some ways, it almost seemed inviting. If the jellyhoppers were going to escape and raid stores and mix them up in burglaries, the responsibility of caring for the creatures was becoming too great.

"Listen to him!" said Jamie, rolling his eyes as Reuben's complaints were made loudly.

"You should have woken me up! You should have! It's not fair!" Reuben pouted.

Ruth's voice answered. "If you complain, I'm not telling you the rest. Now just listen!"

Jamie pulled open the door, and Isobel heard him draw in his breath as she slipped in behind him. Her eyes adjusted quickly to the dimness as Jamie shut the door behind her. She saw almost immediately what had made Jamie gasp, and she didn't have to count to know that now there were sixty-five jellyhoppers in the barn. They both stood, staring into the half-dark barn that glowed with the red and yellow and green shapes of the strange creatures inside. The strange creatures from space that kept on multiplying by some means the children didn't understand.

Finally Jamie spoke. "Maybe it's the chocolate that makes them increase. Perhaps we shouldn't have fed them chocolate."

For a moment or two, Isobel let herself glory in the kaleidoscope of color moving in the barn. "Wow – they are beautiful! And look at their eyes shining! So many eyes!"

"I'm going to take some photos," said Jamie, and before Isobel could ask the question in her mind, Jamie answered it. "My camera's got an automatic flash. And then we should have a meeting and decide everything properly."

Reuben was deeply offended that he had missed out on the night adventure. He refused to sit down with the others for the meeting. "I already decided that we should tell the adults. I said so right at the start, but no one would listen." He stomped off to the barn doorway. "And I said they might take over, and they are."

"Sixty-five hoppers can't take over the world, Reuben," said Ruth crossly. Isobel recognized that while Ruth was irritated by his sulkiness, she was also trying to prevent Reuben from feeling frightened. "Brown's Poultry Farm has more than sixty-five hens – heaps more – and the hens haven't taken over the world, have they?"

"They don't keep multiplying by two all the time, do they?" Reuben disappeared into the barn, clutching a large, blank notepad – for he was fascinated by the creatures' photocopying abilities. Being in a huff wasn't going to prevent him from enjoying that.

"I liked the message you left me," said Ruth to Isobel, remembering the words repeated in soft, shining red.

"That was only yesterday," mused Isobel. "Doesn't it seem like ages since then?"

"It's because so much seems to be happening," said Ruth. "But am I wiped out today! We didn't get home till late, and then we were up half the night. I got such a fright at first when I heard you outside. I thought it was part of a dream."

"I was scared your mother or father was going to come out and find me! Hey, I like your room with the doors that open out onto the yard. It's really great."

Ruth smiled shyly at Isobel. "Would you like to come and stay the night? There's an extra bed in my room."

"I saw it," said Isobel, and happiness fizzed and floated inside her. Ruth wanted her to come and stay! Overnight! They could talk all night, looking out the doors at the moonlight on the yard. They could talk about yesterdays and, better still, about all the tomorrows to come.

"Only if you want to come," said Ruth. Isobel, unsure of Ruth's friendship, had been careful not to say too much about herself when she talked with Ruth at first. (Was it only a day or two ago?) Now, here was Ruth showing the same sort of wariness.

Isobel looked into Ruth's shyly smiling face. "I'd love to come and stay. I'd really love to." She felt her happiness would have to burst out of her somehow, so Isobel flung herself into a series of cartwheels on the grass.

"Wow!" cried Ruth.

"You do it, too. Come on!" shouted Isobel.

Jamie, who had been studiously writing in

his record book, looked up suddenly. "Come on, you two. We have to have our meeting."

The two girls tumbled across the sun-warmed grass, reaching Jamie's feet to lie in two, happy heaps

"Yes, Master," mocked Ruth, in a robotic voice.

Jamie, sitting on the log by the barn wall, stared over them, as though they were too silly to even notice, and said formally, "I have recorded the fact that even the smell of chocolate is enough to draw the hoppers for a long distance. I have also entered, on the diary page, that there are now double the number again."

Ruth sat up. "Have you written about their trip to the store on that page, and about how we got them to come back?"

"Yes, you should write all about it," agreed Isobel. "So that there's a record that's kind of like proof."

"First, let's decide about telling about the hoppers," said Jamie. "I've been thinking about it, and it's sort of hard to know what to do. Will we tell our parents? Will we tell Sheriff O'Shea? Will we tell the scientists? And will any of them listen if we just tell them? So, will we decide who to tell and bring them here and *show* them, rather than *tell* them?"

"We'll have to show someone. You're right," said Isobel. "They won't believe us otherwise. We could just show them one to start with. Maybe Obadiah. Then they'd have to believe it – and then we could show them the rest."

"Who? But who will we show?" asked Ruth.

"I think we should show the scientists. They're still in town," said Jamie.

"And at the same time," said Ruth, her voice excited by the power of the thought that had just occurred to her, "we can tell them that if they are going to be kind to him, we'll show them the rest. If they're not, we won't show them."

"Yes!" agreed Isobel.

"Don't be stupid," said Jamie. "Once we've shown them one, we have to show them the rest, and we can't make them do, or not do, anything – even if we want to."

Ruth and Isobel joined him in a gloomy silence.

Eventually, Jamie said, "OK. In the morning. Tomorrow morning. Today, we'll find out where the scientists are, and I'll finish writing up this book. I might take some more photos, too."

"Let's take some photos with us all in them," said Ruth. "All of us and the jellyhoppers."

"Yes," said Isobel. "All of us sitting among the hoppers."

They all knew that something strange and amazing was coming to an end.

Isobel laughed. "We can sell the photos to the papers and get rich! It's not that bad, is it? We might be world famous! We probably will be!"

Chapter 15

Isobel took Obadiah home that night. It would be the last night he could spend in her bedroom.

"And then what will happen to you, you funny creature? You creature-machine." Isobel patted his warm, shining sleekness, and let him slide over her hands and her feet.

"Your eyes are the only part of you that seems normal – and they don't even blink. I wonder what the scientists are going to think of you. You could be mentioned in history books, you know. In history books of the earth, as the first alien creature to come to this planet. I could be mentioned there, too, along with Jamie and Ruth and Reuben. Of course, there is the chance that they'll forget about us and give the credit to the scientists or some other adults.

"But we found you, and we know that. Ruth and I are going to write a book about it when we grow up. We're going to call it 'The Discovery of the First Space Creatures.' We're going to make it dramatic and exciting, and everyone in the world will want to buy it."

Isobel went to bed early, with Obadiah happily under the sheets, too. She tried, as she had done before, to see if his eyes changed in the dark by lifting the sheets suddenly and peering into the blackness. She couldn't decide whether there was any difference and, exhausted by the previous night's adventures, she soon fell deeply asleep.

Later that night, Obadiah woke her. He wasn't just humming with excitement as he usually did – and even if he had been, she felt that wouldn't have woken her, as she was so tired. He was squeaking. At first the noise seemed very distant, as though it was part of a dream. Isobel blinked and fumbled her head and hands from beneath the sheets, trying to focus on the strange sound.

Obadiah was hopping around the room very fast. With each hop came a strange, high-pitched squeak.

"Stop it. Stop it," she grumbled, too tired to feel surprised by the unusual noise. "Obadiah, I want to go to sleep. Quit it."

The squeaking and hopping went on, as though Obadiah was excited beyond measure. For a moment or two, Isobel had the vague notion that she didn't care if her father was awakened and came into the room. Then she knew she couldn't let that happen – it would interfere with what had been arranged for tomorrow. Also, she couldn't bear the thought of a hundred questions and having to give long explanations. All she wanted to do was sleep.

She tumbled out of bed and managed to get her feet into her sandals. "Out!" she hissed, opening the bedroom door.

Obadiah was down the stairs ahead of her and was waiting at the back door when she reached it. She scooped him up and opened the door, intending to take him down the yard to the shed. But he wriggled violently, slithered from her grasp, and was off, hopping as fast as she had ever seen him move. The squeaks still echoed at every hop, and Isobel thought, although wasn't sure, that she could hear a more distant, yet similar sound.

Isobel groaned. She was so tired. She couldn't bear the thought of chasing Obadiah through the night. She couldn't bear the thought of another chocolate store raid. She couldn't bear to cross fields in the dark and seek out help from her friends. She was tired, tired, tired.

Isobel shut the door and stumbled back up the stairs. He could stay outside, the crazy creature. He could raid stores on his own, for the barn door was firmly shut, and the others couldn't get out unless someone opened it. He could miss out on being the first space creature seen by the scientific world, and they would choose another hopper from the collection in the barn. She was going to bed.

Then, tiptoeing through the door of her bedroom, Isobel felt a sudden stab of guilt mixed with real sorrow. Obadiah was special and rare and amazing – and she had let him escape her grasp without even caring about it. She felt more awake. Should she go out after him now?

She pulled back the curtain, peered out into the night, and shuddered at the shadowed world. She didn't want to go out alone. Last night she had had little time to think about it. Tonight she did, and thinking didn't make the shadows shrink at all. The night was warm, but much cloudier than last night. There was hardly any starlight at all.

Isobel heard a faint humming and turned, staring around the room behind her. Surely Obadiah hadn't come back of his own accord, and followed her up the stairs? She knew the thought was silly. She peered outside instead, searching the gloom for a faint glow of green. The humming came from above. Isobel searched the sky. She couldn't see a thing.

She tiptoed out of her room and slipped through the doorway that led into the spare room where the window faced the other way, out over the back lawn, toward the fields beyond. She opened the window and heard the hum, still there – faint, but still there.

Then she saw it. Something coming low out of the sky, over the field. The shape was too poorly lit by its few lights to make it clear. She was quite unable to describe it later. But she knew, knew without a shadow of doubt, that the shape was not that of a meteorite, or an airplane, or any other thing made by humans.

And she knew something else. She knew that the excited noise Obadiah had made was because of this shape from the sky and that the sound – like his squeaking – had doubtless caused a similar excitement in the distant barnful of jellyhoppers.

She smiled to herself. Were there now one hundred and twenty-nine jellyhoppers out there? Or still just sixty-five? Would the pilots of the alien craft be surprised by their number, or would they have been expecting the increase?

There was one other thing that Isobel knew as she watched the ill-defined shape hover for a few seconds over the field, and then rise high into the air and disappear beyond the clouds – its humming sound going with it. She knew that Obadiah and all the other jellyhoppers were on board. She knew with the same conviction that she knew her own name. Strangely, it didn't really matter.

"You never belonged here, jellyhoppers. You'll be better off at home."

Isobel tiptoed out of the spare bedroom and back into her own. She lay awake a short while, puzzling, remembering. Then she slept.

Morning Star

Established 1919 — Volume LXXVI

CHILDREN SIGHTED NEAR RIBBONWOOD BURGLARY

RIBBONWOOD. A witness to the robbery of Mrs. Wynard's chocolate shop on July 11 alleges he saw three children in the area, at around the time of the break-in.

The source, who wishes to remain unidentified, told police he was on West End Road at around 2:10 a.m. yesterday. He had been visiting a friend, and was walking toward his car when he claims he saw three children carrying a large box, and coming from the direction of Mrs. Wynard's store. The onlooker was unable to name the children.

The chocolate store was burglarized at around 2:00 a.m. on Thursday, July 11. All chocolates in stock were taken, along with some cash.

"I can't understand why all the money wasn't taken," said Mrs. Wynard. "It is almost as though the burglars were frightened away by someone or something. Maybe they were children."

Chapter 16

Meeting time at the barn was to be 9:30 a.m. Isobel was there at nine, and she opened the doors that had been tightly shut the day before. The barn was totally empty, as she knew it would be.

She wondered who or what had opened the doors to let the sixty-four hoppers out and found herself glancing up, as if the mysterious craft was about to return so that the "who" or "what" would take her skyward, too. The barn was now like any other empty barn, big and barren, dusty and bare. It was as if the jellyhoppers had never existed. She loitered awhile, wondering what the inhabitants on the jellyhoppers' planet would make of the pictures and writing that some of the hoppers would reproduce. Would they think panda bears were people? Would they be able to translate writing? Maybe Jamie's record book would be produced on another planet. Would they be able to read the message "WE ARE YOUR FRIENDS" – which was Reuben's way of ensuring his safety? In spite of the other children reassuring him, he had always worried that the jellyhoppers would suddenly escape to an alien place – and then maybe return, guiding alien kidnappers! The jellyhoppers had escaped – or perhaps, more correctly, they had been taken.

It would be better if she told Jamie, Ruth, and Reuben about the departure of the jellyhoppers than let them discover the empty barn. Isobel wandered up to the gate leading into their backyard and waited for them there.

The three children received her story with the same calm acceptance Isobel had felt while watching only part, yet knowing all, of the unexpected night departure. At the same time, all four children felt a definite sense of confusion.

Jamie was the most upset, for he had become excited about revealing their amazing secret to the scientists, and then the world. He had spent a lot of his evening perfecting his record book, planning his words of introduction and explanation. He had even imagined, although he didn't tell the others, what it would be like appearing on television.

"I wish I didn't believe you, but I know it's true," he moaned. "No one would believe us now if we told them, would they? How can we live the rest of our lives knowing what we know without telling anyone? How can we?"

Reuben couldn't help himself. "We should

have told at the beginning."

"REUBEN!" Three voices dared him to say another word.

"Being all ready to tell everyone everything, it seems sort of depressing not to be able to do it," said Ruth. "I'd gotten prepared." She looked at Isobel. "Hadn't you?"

"Yes, I had. And I think we might still have to, even though the hoppers are gone."

The four of them were staring into the empty barn as they talked, and now both Jamie and Ruth stared at Isobel.

"What do you mean?"

"Why would we have to?"

"Didn't you see this morning's paper?" Isobel asked. "The article doesn't have headlines as big as the space stories did, but it wasn't hard to notice it on the front page."

"What article?"

"Someone saw John Rogers in the night and told the police," Isobel continued. "Then John Rogers told the police that he saw three children out that night, and the article makes it sound as if everyone thinks that the three children robbed the chocolate shop."

Jamie had gone quiet and tense, as he did when he was totally unsure of what to do next. Ruth spoke. "We're the three children."

"Uh-huh..." said Isobel. "Except John Rogers said he didn't know who we were. Does he know any of you?"

"I don't know," said Ruth. "I suppose he had to say he saw us because if people think he's making up stories about the spacecraft, they might think he's making up stories about the robbery. He's probably scared that people will think he burglarized the store."

"The police will know by now that it's not John Rogers, and it's not any of you three that robbed the store," said Reuben with unexpected firmness in his voice.

Ruth looked startled, and then slightly irritated. "Reuben, cut it out."

"They will know," said Reuben firmly. "They will, because of my letter and the photocopy."

Jamie came back to life. "What letter?"

"Well, when you were having your meeting yesterday and I was photocopying with the hoppers, some of them made copies of things from in the store – labels and things like that."

"Did they?" said Ruth, suddenly interested.

"And one – it was Obadiah, actually – made a copy of a driver's license. The name on it was Albert James Henward. And you said, Ruth, that one of the men went racing back for something, and you saw him stuffing a card of some kind in his pocket when he came out. I bet it was the driver's license."

"How do you know what a driver's license looks like?" asked Isobel.

"He does know," answered Jamie. "His father was showing him his just the other day. What is the letter you're talking about? You said 'my letter'"

"Well, I wrote a letter," said Reuben. "Just a short one. And I told the police that they should ask this person about the burglary." He made swallowing movements in an effort to stop the smile of pride that kept trying to appear on his face. "It was just like in the books I've read, about kids solving crimes. I wasn't even there, but I still worked it out, and now you're all saved!"

Isobel, Ruth, and Jamie stared in silence at Reuben for a few seconds. Then, one after another, they fired remarks at him.

"You sent the police a photocopy in that strange, shiny red!"

"Didn't you think they might wonder what sort of machine could do that?"

"You wrote them a letter without asking us about it?"

"Just when we had all agreed to see the scientists first!"

Reuben protested, "It would have worked. We were going to see the scientists first thing this morning, and the police won't get the mail until about half-past ten. See?"

"And I suppose," said Jamie, "you wanted the police officers to pat you on the head for being so smart. So I guess you signed your name on the letter."

"Of course I did," said Reuben. "It's very rude to send letters without names. I remember our teacher talking about it once..." His voice trailed off as he realized that Jamie's withering glance was directed at him.

"Woweee!" said Isobel. "You sure were very helpful, Reuben."

The four children sat in silence for awhile, thoughts whirling in every head as they wondered which way to turn now. Jamie got up and started pacing around. Reuben rolled over in the grass, covering his face with his arms. Ruth put an arm around him.

"I think you were really smart to figure that out, Reuben. I don't think I even know what a driver's license looks like."

"When I first found Obadiah, it was like a real adventure, having such a secret," said Isobel. "It's been really different from the way I thought it would be."

"Sure has," agreed Ruth.

"But anyway," said Isobel, "we've got our record book, and we've got the photos. Wow! I'd forgotten about them! Hey, Jamie, we've got the photos! And all of us must stick together. They will believe us – they have to – when we all tell the same story and show the photos. And John Rogers will tell them what he saw, too!"

"Maybe," called Jamie over his shoulder, "or even Albert what's-his-name, and his friends."

"Jamie looks happier now that we've remembered about the photos," said Ruth.

Isobel smiled in agreement. "Anyway, I don't care what happens. It's been really strange, this whole week, really strange. I wonder what my father is going to say when he hears about it. I can't imagine what Mrs. Hopgood will say! You know, if it hadn't been for the hoppers, I wouldn't have met all of you, would I? I asked Dad about coming to sleep over and he said I can, when he's talked to your mother to make sure it's OK with her."

"Great," said Ruth.

Reuben rolled over and sat up. "I'm sorry if I did the wrong thing. I was trying to help."

Jamie stopped pacing. "It's OK, Reuben. It wasn't really the wrong thing. In fact, you were probably the one who was right in the first place. We should have told when we first found the hoppers."

"Doesn't matter," said Ruth, seeing Jamie's

worried frown returning. "Like Isobel says, we'll all stick together and just tell them what happened. One way or another, we're going to be famous, all right!"

"I've never had my picture in the paper," said Reuben.

"You can stand in the front and hold our record book," grinned Jamie. "I've put a name in red, yellow, and green on the front – 'The Week of the Jellyhoppers.' Know what we're going to do now? Go to the one-hour photo store and get the photos developed, and then we're not going to the scientists or the police. We'll go straight to the *Morning Star*!"

The Mor

Sunday, July 14

Establi

RIBBONWOOD C
ALIEN EN

RIBBONWOOD. Four local children – Jamie Anderson (12), Ruth Newton (10), Reuben Newton (8), and Isobel Miro (10) – claim to have experienced an encounter with extraterrestrial beings.

The children visited the *Morning Star* offices yesterday and made an announcement to reporters, alleging that they had discovered a number of unidentifiable creatures on July 6, the day after a UFO sighting was reported in Ribbonwood. Jamie Anderson said that they thought the small, round, brightly colored creatures they found – which they named "jellyhoppers" – were from the UFO, which he believed was

Pictured above are the four children, from left to right: Isobel Miro, Jamie Anderson, Ruth Newton, and Reuben Newton.

ing Star

1919   **Volume LXXVI**

HILDREN CLAIM
COUNTER

Reuben Newton is displaying the record book documenting the encounter titled, "The Week of the Jellyhoppers."

some sort of spacecraft.

Star reporters initially dismissed the report as a childish prank, but had to reconsider the claim when the children produced startling evidence.

Photographs of the four young people with the "jellyhoppers," and a book of recorded observations made by Jamie Anderson, led to further investigation of the claim.

Two experts are at present examining the photographs. Their inquiry is not yet complete, but they have stated that if the photographs are a hoax, they are incredibly authentic-looking.

TITLES IN THE SERIES

SET 9A

Television Drama
Time for Sale
The Shady Deal
The Loch Ness Monster Mystery
Secrets of the Desert

SET 9B

To JJ From CC
Pandora's Box
The Birthday Disaster
The Song of the Mantis
Helping the Hoiho

SET 9C

Glumly
Rupert and the Griffin
The Tree, the Trunk, and the Tuba
Errol the Peril
Cassidy's Magic

SET 9D

Barney
Get a Grip, Pip!
Casey's Case
Dear Future
Strange Meetings

SET 10A

A Battle of Words
The Rainbow Solution
Fortune's Friend
Eureka
It's a Frog's Life

SET 10B

The Cat Burglar of Pethaven Drive
The Matchbox
In Search of the Great Bears
Many Happy Returns
Spider Relatives

SET 10C

Horrible Hank
Brian's Brilliant Career
Fernitickles
It's All in Your Mind,
   James Robert
Wing High, Gooftah

SET 10D

The Week of the Jellyhoppers
Timothy Whuffenpuffen-
   Whippersnapper
Timedetectors
Ryan's Dog Ringo
The Secret of Kiribu Tapu Lagoon